OPEN THE GATE

Move into a life of infinite possibilities

JILL HEALY-QUINTARD

Body and Balance

Disclaimer

This book is presented as a source of information and education. The author, publishers and marketers of this information disclaim any loss or liability, either directly or indirectly as a consequence of applying the information presented herein, or in regard to the use and application of said information.

The information provided is based on over 40 years experience in the fitness industry, the use of which is solely at your own risk.

Please consult your physician or other health care professional before starting this or any other fitness program. Body and Balance explicitly disclaim any and all liability that may result from following the program recommendations made within this book.

Copyright © 2023 by Jill Healy-Quintard.

All rights reserved worldwide. No part of this publication may be replicated, redistributed, or given away in any form without the prior written consent of the author/publisher or the terms relayed to you herein.

Jill Healy-Quintard,
Manly Vale, NSW, 2093, Australia

bodyandbalance.com.au

eISBN: 978-0-646-86838-7
ISBN: 978-0-6459364-0-7

ABOUT THE AUTHOR

Jill is a multi award winning specialist in the field of mind/body connection and personal transformation. She is an advocate for the benefit of human movement and mindfulness which she includes in all of her programs. She is passionate about diversity, equity and embracing multi culturalism, and through the work she's done in the fitness and wellness areas for over 40 years, Jill has helped thousands of men, women and children to improve their wellbeing, and reach goals of all kinds including achieving a sense of balance in their life.

She is a sought after speaker and presenter who offers presentations, classes and training. Her ground breaking program called "Keeping Your Working Body and Mind Fit" is particularly popular with Corporates and Schools alike.

Jill's first book called *YogaPilates Fusion: A Mind Body and Balanced Practice* was released in 2019. It focused on Jill's 10 Principles of Wellbeing that she developed over 35 years in the industry.

In this book "Open the Gate", Jill shares aspects of her life that informed the approach she takes to educating others in strategies to transform their life.

CONTENTS

INTRODUCTION	1
One MY STORY	11
Two THE CARE WE GIVE OURSELVES	23
Three THE WORLD WE LIVE IN	34
Four THE BODY WE LIVE IN	43
Five THE FOOD WE EAT	52
Six BRAIN AND GUT HEALTH	67
Seven THE EXERCISE WE DO	74
Eight THE RELATIONSHIPS WE FORM	123
CONCLUSION	139
APPENDIX I: Shortcuts to Being Well	141
APPENDIX II: Case Studies	145

OPEN THE GATE

INTRODUCTION

This book is all about helping you to create a path to sustainable wellbeing in mind and body. I will walk with you and be your ally the whole way, but I can't do the work for you. That's as it should be, because while the results you'll be working towards will feel fantastic once you've achieved them, it's the effort you put in to achieving your goals that will open you up to the potential for personal growth that will support your physical and emotional wellbeing for the rest of your life.

In 2023 as I'm writing these words, being emotionally, physically, and spiritually well is even more important and even more challenging than it was when I published my first book called *Yoga Pilates Fusion* in 2019. I say that because of the competing agendas and fissures in our sense of community that I see as the legacy of a whole lot of tensions that were exacerbated by the Covid-19 pandemic. I've chosen not to go into those things here, except to note that we live in challenging times.

That said, we can equip ourselves to be well no matter what's going on around us. That's the theme you will find running through this book.

I come to you from a place of deep commitment to pro-ageing and personal empowerment. My approach is based on balancing the mind and body to increase your longevity. This perspective runs parallel to the anti-ageing industry. Mine is a deeper more positive approach that offers you the opportunity to have more fun and achieve sustainable success on the journey to changing your behaviours around the food you eat, the exercise you do, and the amount of love you give yourself on a daily basis.

The decades I've spent in the fitness, health and wellbeing industries have made two things very clear to me. The first one is that respecting the connection between the mind and body is integral to our ability to be well. The second one is that taking control of our future starts with firstly becoming aware of, and then adjusting any mindset patterns that are likely to sabotage our results.

I give you strategies to maintain a positive mindset in this book because one of the things that really worries me about the world we live in is that most people give their power away to a medical system that is based on the inevitability of declining health as we age. This runs counter to my approach which is to empower people like you to be positive and optimistic about the wonderful future they will have once they put the proper foundations in place. Those foundations are not only based on being positive and optimistic, they're also about acting on the advice I provide in this book. The bottom line is that having a healthy relationship with ourselves backed up by a robust mindset is integral to maintaining these foundations.

Right off the bat, I want to say that the key to being positive and optimistic is to reorientate your thinking so that you can enjoy who you are, no matter what stage of life you are in. As you move through this book, I'll be reminding you to laugh, to love and to have fun. I'll also be inviting you to join my online community of women who are taking the power around their health and their life back into their own hands.

What you'll find in the chapters that follow are strategies that will ease you in to feeling comfortable about making strategic changes that will predispose you to be fit and well right up until the time you die. My experience is that the majority of people over 40 don't look forward to their future. This is because they've bought into the stereotype of having to endure a painful and unhappy period of years or even decades before they leave their body behind. Sadly, I often hear people saying things like, "Oh well, I have to expect pain in my knees because I'm getting older." This drives me nuts because it doesn't have to be that way.

By reading this book and implementing what you learn in the process, you will be positioning yourself to beat the odds and enjoy the rest of your life with an abundance of health and a true wealth of spirit.

It makes me incredibly proud to be sharing my story and the stories of some of the hundreds of people I've worked with over the years. I share these so you can see that 'real' people just like you have been able to turn their life around. Many of them have come from a place of adversity and pain and worked their way through to a place of continual improvement in relation to their health and their wellbeing overall. For example, you'll be hearing about how I overcame issues with boundaries on the mindset front, and how I healed myself in record time after a double hip replacement, to now being a woman in her mid-sixties who revels in her ability to inspire and coach others to do what they need to be truly well and take their life to a whole other level.

The stories I share show a determination to delve into some possibly difficult emotional territory that you've probably been avoiding for a very long time. I would like you to do that yourself because there is so much to be gained through identifying any negative beliefs that have had a hand in shaping the person you are today. What you'll be doing by coming to terms with the extent to which you have limited your thinking about what you can and cannot achieve, is opening the gate to a whole new future for yourself. What I want to do is support you to get real and be prepared to make some changes if it turns out that you've been short-changing yourself because you are stuck in patterns that are limiting your ability to access the life of infinite possibility that is waiting for you.

Imagine what it would be like if you had the tools to peel back the surface layers of who you are so that you can feel into what you need to do to embody your life's full potential. If you're the kind of person who likes to highlight important points in a book, then I want you to stop reading now and find a highlighter. I want you to do that so that you can run it across the last word in this sentence, because what I'm here to tell you is that the most important tool you need at your disposal is awareness. It's awareness that will enable you to get clear about what you need to do to take your wellbeing to a whole other level. And together, we are going to expand your awareness and explore specific areas of fitness and wellness that will enable you to develop a set of positive intentions to get to where you want to be.

Before we go on this journey together, I want you to know why you should listen to me. I've been involved in the fields of fitness and wellness for over 40 years. I've helped thousands of men, women and children to reach their health, wellness and fitness potential, either through my face-to-face or online group classes, or through working on a one-on-one basis with me.

My proudest achievements to date include being recognised for my contribution to innovation in the fields of health and wellness at the Women's Economic Forum in India in 2017. I was also nominated in the Top 5 and Top 3 Group Fitness Instructors in the Australian Fitness Industry in 2019 and 2020 respectively, as well as being offered the inaugural Lifetime Member Award by Barrie Elvish the CEO of AUSactive (formally Fitness Australia) in 2021. In 2022 I was nominated in four categories in the AUSactive Fitness Awards and won National Pilates Professional of the Year and National Yoga Business of the Year. I feel particularly honoured to have recently taken a judging position with AUSactive for the awards in other categories to my own, and am now a finalist in 2 categories in the 2023 awards.

I'm incredibly proud of the feedback I receive from people who work through the program I included in my international best-selling book *YogaPilates Fusion: A Mind Body and Balanced Practice*, as well as those who took part in my *Yoga Pilates Fusion: Power, Breath, Intention* workshop that I ran for hundreds of delegates at the Filex Fitness Convention in Sydney in 2019. In fact, being chosen to present my unique methods to this group of professionals is a testament to my standing in an industry that tends to be dominated by 'young' people. I love being a walking talking beacon of hope for anyone who wants the last half of their life to be as good, if not better, than the first.

I started writing this book prior to the Covid-19 pandemic that took the world by storm in 2020. I returned to my home base in Australia at the end of 2019 after a journey with my husband travelling through France, Spain, Morocco and Vietnam. One thing I know for sure is that magical things can happen when we take ourselves out of our comfort zone. Travelling is certainly not the only way to do that, however on this occasion, taking myself to places where I could refresh my perspective gave me the opportunity to recognise that I had essentially been giving myself a hard time for not being good enough for decades.

Words can't express how empowering it has been to finally stop believing the illusion I had been buying into about what success looks like, and just start believing in myself 100%. Sure, I still have doubt from time to time, but these days I'm much better at being able to acknowledge and then ignore the negative little voice in my head and keep moving toward my goals regardless.

If you get nothing else out of this book, I want you to know that negative self-talk is one of the most destructive forces there is. It will totally undermine your wellbeing if you let it run free. I share this with you because there is nothing wrong with you if you find yourself repeating unhelpful patterns over and over again. It is actually natural. That doesn't mean it's ok though. My hope is that reading about what I've been through in the way of personal transformation over the years will help you to see that almost anything is possible when you take your mindset-related challenges on, rather than sweeping them under the carpet.

I was excited to get back to Australia and start a fresh year in 2020 with a new sense of optimism. In particular, I felt buoyed by the fact that Australia was out the other side of the catastrophic season of bushfires that ravaged the country at the end of 2018 and continued through the beginning of 2019. The fires destroyed thousands of people's homes and livelihoods, and decimated untold numbers of precious wildlife. We had a short period of relief when the long-awaited rains broke the terrible drought that had made the country so susceptible to bushfires in the first place. Then suddenly the World Health Organisation informed us that we were heading into a worldwide pandemic of unknown proportions.

I find it interesting to note that as we've entered another chapter in relation to the pandemic, a lot of previously silent and compliant voices are coming to the fore with alternative narratives to counter the fact that we're still being bombarded with negative doom and gloom from our politicians and the mainstream media. As I see it, more and more people have decided to switch off and make up their own minds about what they should and shouldn't do when it comes to their wellbeing. It feels to me like the idea that each of us needs to take responsibility for doing what it takes to grow and transform through these times we're living in now is starting to gain some traction.

I guess I could sum all of this up by saying that we live in strange and challenging times, and now more than ever it's important for people like us to be clear headed as well as being physically and emotionally strong. Even though Australia has been relatively unscathed compared to our counterparts in the US and the UK, we are still seeing businesses going to the wall and people losing their jobs at levels that are up there with the worst times in our country's history.

Among other things, we are seeing increasing numbers of people working from home and adjusting to this 'new normal' in various constructive ways. I personally found the Covid period to be a strangely positive time, where people were inclined to slow down and reflect on what really matters to them as they found new ways to work, play and enjoy life.

Meanwhile some things never seem to change. For example, it never ceases to amaze me how adept the wonderful women who come to me for help are at undermining their confidence by believing they are 'not good enough'. Although I guess I shouldn't be too amazed because not so long ago I was one of those women myself. I know from first-hand experience that whether our 'not good enough' thinking plays out in terms of not being pretty enough, or strong enough, or smart enough, or skinny enough, or blond enough, or popular enough, or whatever, the bottom line is that these beliefs are just stories we tell ourselves to be able to stay small.

You might be wondering why on earth we would want to stay small. I know that logically it makes no sense at all, but somewhere along the way people like us are likely to pick up the idea that to be safe we must keep our head down and stay small. So right now, let me tell you this is not true. The truth is that you will only ever be as safe as you allow yourself to believe you are. What's more, you always have a choice about whether to buy into the stories that drive a wedge between you and the wonderful life you are entitled to, or the stories that highlight all of the ways in which you are absolutely good enough.

I want to acknowledge that I picked up plenty of my own emotional baggage growing up as a baby boomer through the 1960's in Australia. This was a time where feminism was in its infancy, and the blokey values of the time were bearing down on me every single day of my life. Even though that was the case, you'll be hearing about how an inner rebelliousness that I inherited from my mother led to my being able to manifest a wonderful life as a feminist, a hippy, a creative, an academic, a wife, a parent and a pro-aging woman who is passionate about doing whatever I can to help as many women as possible to rise to the challenge of increasing the fitness of their mind and their body so that they can be happy and well.

Open The Gate is a book of empowerment, motivation, information, and self-exploration - both for you and for me. To my great surprise the act of writing this book turned out to be an incredibly healing experience. I've done a lot of study and personal development work on myself over the years. I've gained diplomas in teaching, acting and massage therapy, and completed many courses in healing and movement, but I still managed to uncover long hidden mindset patterns that were stopping me from taking my life to the next level.

I don't mind telling you that it was confronting for me to own that fact, and to launch into the uncomfortable territory of disentangling what was really going on. However, I pushed on because I've been in the wellbeing game for long enough to know that I've had a 'calling,' and that it is my life's purpose to empower people to create their best life no matter what age they are. To that end, I'm committed to being true to my own ideals without flinching. What that means is that I will be telling you everything that's relevant about my life with raw honesty and integrity. That's only fair because this book is my invitation for you to take a deep dive into your soul, and to interrogate your mindset so that you can stop running interference on yourself. This matters because it's well past time for you to start doing the important work of nurturing and loving yourself that you might not have ever been taught how to do.

A key player in my story is my mother. In fact, it's her story that gave rise to the title of this book. You'll hear more about this later, but for now, I just want to acknowledge that my mother is the one who is responsible for introducing me to an environment that led to a life-long appreciation of the power of dance and music. These were the things that resonated with me and grounded me when I was a little girl, and they still do to this day. I have combined that background with a passion for fitness and wellness and bundled everything I know into this book to show you how to open your mind and your body to the infinite possibilities that we all have within us.

I've organised this book in this way because I want to help you to understand that the life you are living now is determined by your current belief system. I want to show you what you can achieve by changing any lifestyle practices that are generated by a mindset that is compromising your ability to be well. I go right back to the very basics of explaining what our body needs to function at its best. I provide this information as a framework for you to fully understand the opportunities to increase your wellbeing.

In fact, the impetus for this book came from the feedback I receive from the clients I work with. It really warms my heart when I hear about how much better these people feel when they implement the strategies I share with them. Because of course, implementation is key to getting the results you want. I had a real wakeup call when I received some feedback from a woman called Judith Roberts who was visiting Australia from the UK in 2019. She said, "Your classes are the best I have done in the entire world, and I want to be able to follow you wherever I am." That was when the penny dropped, and I realised the time had come for me to step up onto a bigger stage and have a more global impact with my empowering pro-aging message.

My sense of the state of things mid 2023 as I'm putting the finishing touches on this book, is that the world is beckoning women like me to up-level our influence and not only support other women, but also to support the men in our lives to find the part of themselves that doesn't need to be macho and unemotional in order to feel empowered.

I don't know if you've heard people talking about the divine feminine rising. What I want to say about that is that it's not about women ruling the world. Rather it's about authentic female and male voices being heard in a world that values collaboration over competition, and positivity over negativity. If we all play our part, I believe it will finally be possible for us to move forward in a more sustainable and healthful way and achieve a higher level of peace and balance in the world.

Obviously, this won't necessarily be plain sailing. One thing I can't help but notice is an alarming rise in the incidence of depression across the board. My way of doing what I can to help here includes running online and offline YogaPilates and Yoga Nidra programs to skill people up in managing stress, anxiety and depression, along with the more general programs I run to nurture people who are struggling with any area of their life whatsoever. And I'm incredibly proud to have just launched a new elite program for women who are finally ready to step beyond their limiting beliefs and transform themselves into the powerful beings they were born to be.

My motto is 'Shape Your Body, Shape Your Mind' because I believe that mindfulness and balance is the only way to cope in the crazy world we're living in right now. It's a world that places multiple demands on us that can diminish our ability to be well in general, and to age well in particular. The way we work is only one part of the scenario, but I must confess to having a particular passion for helping people who fall victim to one of the biggest problems of the current age known as 'sitting disease'. To this end, I developed a program called *Keeping your Working Body and Mind Fit* for deskbound workers to help them maintain flexibility, stability, and productivity. You can access this and my other programs on my web site: bodyandbalance.com.au.

So to turn the focus squarely back on to you now, this book is about empowering you to become the very best version of yourself that you can be. As you read on, you'll see that I'm not perfect. At best I'm perfectly imperfect just like everybody else. I've laid my trials and tribulations out for you to see because I want you to know that no barriers are too high for people like you and I to get over. I say that because I am living proof that recovery from all kinds of problems is possible. The only difference in my case is that I didn't have someone like me by my side to cut out the noise and help me to focus on what really matters.

I've written this book because I know that not everyone is in the position to work directly via the live one on one or group contexts I offer. If that sounds like the position you are in, I want you to know that I've got your back. And if you should ever need any help at all, you can access the raft of resources that I've developed over the years and made available on my website, bodyandbalance.com.au.

***To protect the privacy of individuals, some names in this book have been changed**

CHAPTER ONE

MY STORY

The title *Open the Gate* was inspired by an experience I had when my mother reached out to me from the grave. It's not the kind of thing that happens every day. On this occasion a group of us who had just finished a Chi Ball training course were relaxing and reflecting on what we'd learnt, and just for a bit of fun we decided to play the supernatural game of Ouija. We weren't really taking it seriously in the beginning, but the mood changed dramatically when the woman next to me grabbed my arm and started saying "open the gate" repeatedly. Then she said "Jill - it's your mother," and went on to tell the group that my mother appeared in the form of a little girl on a horse trying to get through a gate before nightfall because she was worried about losing her horse. I was totally knocked off balance by this, and more than a little bit freaked out, because this was a story that I'd heard before.

The story my mother told me when I was just a little girl revolved around the fact that she lost her beloved horse as punishment for getting home late. This happened because of her father's lack of flexibility around the deadline he set for her to get home by. It makes me incredibly sad to think that my mother took the pain she experienced around this part of her life with her to the grave. Whether you believe in someone's ability to deliver a message from the other side or not, I can assure you that the words spoken to me on that night after the Chi

Ball class were particularly meaningful to me. And the feeling of empowerment I had in that moment has stayed with me to this day.

In a sense, the act of writing this book and thereby putting myself 'out there' feels like the energy of my mother motivating me to break through the barriers that have stopped me from stepping up and having a bigger impact for many, many years. It's as if writing this book is my way of opening the gate to freedom and empowerment for myself, and posthumously for my mother as well. What's more, it is my invitation for you to open the gate for yourself too.

I wasn't very far into the book writing journey before it became obvious that there was one area in my life that had been screaming for attention for a long time. That area was boundaries. I can't tell you how grateful I am that the process of delving into my story forced me to recognise that my boundaries were in a sorry state. This matters because solid boundaries are what we need to protect ourselves from energy vampires and others who are not coming from a place where our best interests are served.

Working through this territory helped me to see that there were several factors that made sense of my habit of letting toxic people stay in my life for way too long. In one case I'd been in deep denial. In another case I'd given in to well entrenched people-pleasing tendencies. And in the case of my apparent inability to just delete the emails I receive from businesspeople who are trying to sell me products that I simply don't need, it became obvious that it was a kind of fear of missing out (FOMO) that was playing out for me. Acknowledging this led to my breaking some old habits that no longer served me so that I could prioritise self-care through the establishment of better boundaries.

So now it's time to turn the focus back on you. And I want to ask you:

- How are your boundaries looking at the moment?
- Is there work that needs to be done to make self-care a priority?
- If so, are you ready to step up and do the work?

- If you're not ready to do it yet, what would need to happen for you to be ready?

Don't worry If you're not sure how to answer these questions. You are in the right place to learn how to put yourself into a state where self-care will start to feel like second nature to you. In fact, there is a whole chapter focussing on this topic coming up.

One thing you should know about me is that everything I do is a celebration of the incredible benefits that come from incorporating a healthy dose of movement and music into our schedule. In fact, it was almost a given that I would go down the fitness and wellness path because I was just a kid when I learnt to love the rush of endorphins that fill our body after we start moving. And because this made so much difference to my life, I started encouraging people to increase their wellbeing through movement well before people like Jane Fonda came onto the scene in the early 1980s. And I've been inventing and reinventing ways to move and strengthen the body and the mind ever since.

As far as I'm concerned, establishing habits that contribute to the goal of being physically and emotionally fit is the only sensible path for people like us to take because I know of no better way to achieve longevity and happiness. I don't present this proposition to you from a position of never having had any practical experience of being unwell. A big part of my story has to do with injury and recovery, not only from physical ailments, but also from emotional ones like depression as well. So I have 'real' credentials when it comes to knowing what it feels like when things don't go our way, and I definitely know how hard it can be to see the forest for the trees when overwhelm and/or self-doubt steals our positivity away.

If there's one thing I know for sure, it's that our quality of life is not about what happens to us. It's about how we choose to respond to the things that happen that matters most. Focussing on what we can learn from adversity and struggle rather than wallowing in victimhood and despair, is what makes us into the empowered people we're meant to be. It takes a particular strength of mind to be able to thrive through difficulties. And that's why I spend time going deep into the question of mindset further on in this book.

I'm going to share relevant parts of my story through this book to give you a sense of why I'm the right person to help you. For example, one part of my story includes recovery from a serious injury I sustained in one of the first ever Hot Yoga Classes held in Sydney in the late 1990's. In this particular case the instructor pushed me much further into a pose than my body could go without being injured. The injury I sustained was a tear in my right labrum. The labrum is a rim of soft tissue that surrounds our hip sockets. Tearing mine was not only incredibly painful, but also incredibly inconvenient at the time. I was the mother of a 5-year-old daughter and an active teenage boy, and I was running a business as well as teaching group fitness and dance classes for adults as well as working with children with disabilities.

The version of myself that turned up day after day back then was determined to push on and push through. I wasn't as self-aware as I am now, and I was determined not to drop any of the balls I had in the air. I guess the saying that 'what doesn't kill you makes you stronger' turned out to be true in some ways. But in acknowledging that, I'm not underestimating the fallout from the way my handling of this situation played out for me. There was a definite downside to the craziness of pushing on and pushing through that I'll tell you about in a moment. But on the upside, I have to say that I found out an awful lot about myself in the process of having to dig deep to heal on both a physical and emotional level after having my first hip replaced.

Overall, what this experience left me with is a determination to do whatever it takes to maintain the best health I possibly can. This entails always treating self-care as a priority. And as many of my clients will tell you, I insist they listen to what their body is telling them, instead of putting their health and wellbeing at risk by following the latest trends and/or buying into the all-too-common spirit of competitiveness that the fitness industry is contaminated with.

When I tell people about the way I continued to work through the pain of my torn labrum for years, they are both amazed and appalled. Looking back on this now I can see that I was only able to override the incredible pain I was in because being in pain wasn't as alien to me as it probably is to most people. That's one of the legacies of spending decades in the dance and fitness worlds where pain is an accepted way of life. The old saying of 'no pain, no gain' made sense to me back then, but I can assure you that it doesn't ring true for me anymore.

In 1998 I moved my young family to France when I wasn't taking my injury as seriously as I should have been. While I was over there, I gained an enviable reputation for my unique approach to crafting exercise routines around a fusion of yoga and Pilates. I brought this legacy along with my personal legacy of pain back to Sydney when we returned. And you guessed it, I jumped right back into the crazy schedules and frenetic energy that my life in Sydney was all about. All the while pretending that I could go on pushing through the pain indefinitely.

Although of course that was never going to work, and eventually my body started to fail me in ways I couldn't ignore anymore. I had a reality check when I eventually got around to seeing a hip surgeon who told me that the only course of treatment available to me at that stage was a total hip replacement.

Incredibly though, I still managed to teach my full suite of *Body and Balance Pilates* classes, as well as juggling the responsibilities of being the Gym Manager for a corporate vitamin company. Looking back on it now, I can't believe I thought it was ok to struggle through the pain of having to get wherever I was teaching my class with the aid of a walking stick, and eventually having to run the sessions from a seated position.

It wasn't only my body that was in pain at this time either. Before too long I started to suffer from severe depression. What was lurking at the back of my mind was an insidious fear about never being totally mobile again. The one bright light in my life was my wonderful husband and family. Seriously, I don't know where I would be today without their support, and the open-minded GP and psychologist who helped me to get through my darkest days.

On a physical level, the reality was that I was in hell. In addition to taking pain killers and anti-inflammatories to maintain my crazy schedule, I was also partying on weekends and drinking way too much. Looking back on it now, it's clear that I was in denial about the toll my lifestyle was taking on my body. Denial can only last for so long though, and a sense of unease around the damage I was doing to my liver and my gut with all the drugs I was putting into my body was starting to hit home. Clearly, I had to find another way to manage the situation.

The other way was pretty extreme because I'd left it so long that the only option was to have surgery to totally replace my right hip. This was a big deal for me. Not only because a part of my body was being replaced with a prosthetic joint in a procedure that would require considerable downtime, but also because we were forced to take out a second mortgage on our house to fund the surgery.

But finances aside, what was really playing on my mind was the terrible toll the degeneration of my hip had taken on my muscle tone. This came about because my cartilage was wearing away over the years that I spent avoiding surgery in the misplaced belief that toughing it out was the way to go. It was awful to see the results I'd achieved from a lifetime spent diligently working my body just wasting away.

Meanwhile I was doing my best to support myself by using alternative therapies including massage, meditation and chiropractic treatments as much as I could. I was determined to be able to avoid putting any more drugs into my body than necessary. Meanwhile I was descending into a deep depression, and I started drinking to numb my pain (both emotional and physical). The other thing that was draining my energy was the effort I was putting in to pretending that I was still the fit and happy person my family and clients knew me to be. Was I doing it for them, or was I doing it for me? I don't really know. What I do know is that I was really scared because it felt like my life was falling apart around me.

Of course, especially where an injury leads to surgery there is a period of rehabilitation to factor in. I feel a bit ill when I think about what the initial stage of my rehabilitation involved. To put this into perspective, you need to know that the surgery I had started with my old hip being smashed. Then a ceramic cup and a titanium stem were inserted into my body. And after about four hours under anaesthetic I was sewn back up again. When I came to, the nurse who was looking after me pulled me up to a standing position with a morphine drip attached to my arm and told me to take my first step.

All I could think of to say was "WTF, no way", but she wasn't going to let me get away with that. And after a bit of arguing I got up and took a step. Then I vomited all over the place. Words don't do justice to the horrific pain I was in. All I really remember is collapsing into the arms of my guardian angel in the shape of the nurse who was looking after me. Her name is Roxanne. She sorted me out after I threw up and got me up again so that I could take some more steps before settling back into bed for some much-needed rest.

That's all I have in the way of detail for you because the days after my operation were a bit of a blur. All I know is that somehow the staff at the hospital continued to get me up and moving. And eventually I started walking with the aid of a frame. Then I graduated to crutches, and then to a walking stick. I went home a week after my surgery and continued to have regular sessions of physio as an out-patient in the heated pool at the hospital. It was only at that point that I started to get my inner spark back, and to my surprise I found myself loving the rehab work.

While the healing process was slow but steady, the miracle was that after about a month I had no more pain in my hip at all. And my body started feeling good when I got back onto my natural therapies. These enabled me to start flushing out the chemicals the drugs I'd been taking had flooded my system with. Also, my chiropractor came to my house and treated me to keep my spine strong, and she gave me some homeopathic drops to use, while my physiotherapist was keeping a close eye on me as well.

Overall, mine was a case of speedy progress toward recovery. Within six weeks from the surgery I was able to go back to my studio. At first, I was there as an observer at the back of the room while my stand-in instructors were leading the classes. Then I eased myself back in by taking a couple of sets of exercises at first, until I was finally able to take a full class on my own again. I felt a great sense of empowerment as I came out the other side of the injury/recovery scenario.

The one thing I knew for sure from that point forward is that our bodies have a truly amazing power to heal. The whole experience really fired up my passion for fitness and wellness because it was clear to me that I only got through the surgery as well as I did because of the level of general fitness I had on my side when I went under the knife.

I had my second hip replaced in 2014. This experience was much easier because I was better prepared. I put my body through a total cleanse before I went into surgery. This included cutting out things like alcohol, and taking more vitamins, minerals, and homeopathic medicines, along with continuing my meditation and exercise routines. I kept all of this up right until the night before the operation. Although there was still pain involved in the post-op period, my healing was much more easeful this time around because I had a significantly more robust mindset on my side. Not to mention the fact that the process had improved in the seven-year period since my first hip was done.

In addition to my regard for physical fitness and mindset, a deep appreciation of the fact that there is a spiritual aspect to all of us is integral to everything I do. For want of a better word, I'm going to call this spiritual aspect our 'soul'. In fact, I was doing a guided meditation a little while back and the voice I was following mentioned the word 'soul'. That word triggered something very deep inside of me. To help you to make sense of this, I need to give you a bit of information about what my early years were like.

My father was a staunch Irish Catholic. True to form he loved nothing more than spending time with his large extended family and having a drink and a laugh with his friends in the pub. My mother on the other hand was a rebel who both believed in and did things that were way ahead of her time. She had no time for Catholicism at all, but it was my father who won the argument about where my sister and I were going to school.

I believe the fact that we wound up being educated in the Catholic system is what led me to tap into an internal rebelliousness to stop my self-esteem and sense of self-determination from going out the window. When all is said and done, I'm left with a deep sense of compassion for the little girl who was rewarded for being the kind of person she was with a well-developed sense of self and a zest for life, by being chastised for almost everything she did to the extent that she came out the other end believing she was a sinner.

In addition to the impact the church had on me during my formative years, the dance world also shaped the way I looked at things. The influence both institutions had on me were filtered through the unconscious messages I took on board through the images I saw (and continue to see) in the media. These images represent a very limited view of what being beautiful, desirable, acceptable, and successful looks like.

You'll be hearing more about what I call the external influences that colour our perception of ourself in the next chapter. But the point I want to make here is that we need to be conscious when it comes to self-care because it's just too easy to buy into notions about not being good enough because we don't conform to the impossible images of 'perfection' that are bandied about all over the place.

One of the most important things I got out of everything that went on in my early years, is a deep understanding of what it means to have a soul. With the wisdom of hindsight and decades of healing and self-care behind me, I now understand that the soul I mentioned earlier reflected the idea of a dirty soul that I was brought up to believe I embodied. My memory of this is at the same time quite funny and very sad. I say that because what I saw in the meditation was the shape of the bottom of a shoe. Specifically, it was the sole of a shoe with dirty marks on it that came to mind. When I reflected on that experience, I realised that what this represented was my internalisation of all the so called 'sins' that I was meant to have committed. Writing this now, I think it's outrageous that (because of the way education was delivered to me) an innocent little girl grew up to be a woman with a distorted impression of her worth based on the deeply ingrained idea that she was dirty and sinful.

Fortunately, my mother was the ballast that kept me afloat. I'm incredibly grateful that she had the wherewithal to provide my sister and I with a much wider range of alternatives than the very limiting ideas that our formal education provided. My mother was a brilliant role model for us. She was well respected as a designer of cutting-edge fashion that was popular with a wild and wonderful clientele in Sydney where we lived. I loved and learnt a lot from all the outrageous things she used to do back in the day. The kinds of things I'm talking about include reading tea leaves and spending time with creative people from the worlds of the performing and visual arts.

One thing my mother told me was that before she even knew she was pregnant with me, a well-known celebrity clairvoyant called Richard Stirling told her that she would have two daughters, and that the older one would be well known for her legs, and the other one would be well known for her hands. He gets a tick for a vague kind of accuracy from me here. I say that because I have always been focussed on movement, dance and fitness, and my sister Kerri Anne Healy is an amazing artist. Kerri is the person who painted the cover image for this book.

My sister and I are particularly close. We recently had a conversation about a disgusting Catholic priest who is now deceased. Among other things he is known to have regularly touched young children inappropriately. The background to this is that priests like the one in question were often invited to family homes for lunches and dinners. I remember feeling particularly uncomfortable with this priest being in our house when my father wasn't there. When I was only eight years old, I had a strong gut feeling that something wasn't right, especially when the priest suggested that he help my sister and me to get into bed.

It still makes my skin crawl when I think about the chilling arrogance of this priest when I asked him what he was doing with his hands under the covers of my sister's bed. The cold evil stare he gave me when he said "I am a priest, a man of god, so don't you dare tell your mother" is etched on my brain. My mother died many years later, never knowing anything about this. And my sister and I carried this shared piece of history around with us in silence for decades. It was only very recently that we brought this out into the open and dissected it together.

The upshot of all of this is that neither of us have any respect for priests or nuns. Their hypocritical preaching and behaviour that we witnessed firsthand is not something we're prepared to accept as being anywhere near appropriate to the level of trust so many people hold the institution they represent in.

As I'm writing this book, I reflect on the appalling legacy of the cover ups in the priesthood that people in power in Australia where I live (and beyond) were inclined to turn a blind eye to. They have so much to answer for when it comes to their responsibility for the psychological damage sustained by the small children in their care who were taken advantage of. I live in hope that all these children managed to grow up to be strong, positive and assertive people. And if they have taken the initiative to seek justice as many have, I hope their voice is being heard and respected in a world where equality plays out with some people being more equal than others.

One important lesson I learnt as a young girl is to never trust anyone or anything that my gut feels isn't quite right. I watched a YouTube video recently where a young musician called Dua Lipa talks about being a female in a male dominated industry. I'm sharing the link to Dua's video with you here. I'd love to hear what you think about what she has to say.

www.youtube.com/watch?v=NICtDIVP5mk

For my own part, by the age of eight I was attending one of the most prestigious ballet schools in Sydney. It may have been prestigious, but it was anything but convenient. My weekly commutes to ballet classes provided me with an education of a whole other kind than my parents intended. As unintended as it was, it had the effect of shaping me in ways that still play out to one degree or other to this day. I smile as I think about the trend toward helicopter parenting that's common these days, vis a vis the fact that before I was even double digits I was travelling by train (usually by myself) all the way from my school in the suburbs, into the ballet school in the city. What I dreaded most was the last leg of the journey where I walked through Hyde Park which was frequented by sleazy old men who tended to flash their genitals at young girls like me.

You'll find more of my story woven through the chapters that follow. What I want to highlight here is the fact that anything that makes a young child feel unsafe or as if they have been betrayed will linger deep inside their psyche until something happens to force it to be dealt with. I of all people know that it's easier said than done to bring our deepest fears and long hidden secrets out into the open. But I know that's exactly what we need to do to get to the bottom of what's holding us back from finding our true purpose in life.

I'm incredibly grateful that the proverbial gate has been opened for me through writing my story down in this book. What's more, I feel privileged to be in the position to show anyone who's up for the journey, how to open their own gate as well. I really hope that you are going to be one of those people.

CHAPTER TWO

THE CARE WE GIVE OURSELVES

"Everybody is a genius, but if you judge a fish by its ability to climb a tree, it will live its life believing it is stupid"
Albert Einstein

If there's one thing I know it's that self-care is fundamental to our health and wellbeing. As I mentioned in the last chapter, the first thing you need to focus on to establish a solid foundation for yourself, is whether you have any mindset related issues that could be compromising your ability to be well. That's where the quote from Einstein comes in. Putting it at the beginning of this chapter is my way of urging you to stop having unreasonable expectations of yourself. It's just not fair that we wind up hating parts of our bodies because they don't stack up against the immaculate photoshopped images of gorgeous 20-year-olds we see on social media.

The idea of self-care means different things to different people. To me it means developing a high level of self-awareness, and a preparedness to change whenever I notice myself slipping back into patterns of thinking and/or behaving that are counterproductive to my goal of being well.

For example, as I mentioned earlier, when I started to write this book I recognised that even after decades of personal development and inner work I'd done on myself, I still had a major issue with boundaries. I decided to exorcise my demons in this regard by voicing and sharing some of the details of a particular problem that had been building up for years.

This only came out of the unconscious part of my mind when I started looking at who I was 'turning up as' in the process of writing this book. That awareness alone might have been enough for me to change the dynamic within this relationship. In other words, I probably didn't need to write about it and share it with you here to be able to shift the energy that had been keeping me stuck, but I decided to share it with you to get you motivated to look into whether there are any issues with boundaries that are playing out in your own life.

Essentially there are four key messages that I want you to take away from this chapter. They are:

1. That it's never too late to start to look after yourself in terms of establishing healthy boundaries.
2. That no matter how much work you think you've done on yourself, it's still possible for entrenched programming to be playing out below the level of your conscious awareness.
3. That no matter how tempting it might be to just brush uncomfortable emotional material under the carpet, the energy we use to repress things is always greater than the energy required to transform and then transcend them.
4. It's worth being open to continuing to evolve throughout life because there is literally no limit to how great our life can be.

Whether you have issues around boundaries or not, if you think about who or what is stopping you from doing what you need to do to thrive, I'm pretty sure you're going to have to admit that the only thing in the way is you. And I know how frustrating it can be to have to deal with this fact, because of course it makes no sense at all that we wouldn't do everything in our power to be as well as we possibly can. So, to help you to make sense of this, I'm going to start to unpick the question of mindset using an edited extract from Jane Turner's book called *Thrive in Midlife*. Jane and I are creative partners. We are both of the view that there's no sense in reinventing the wheel, and I want to acknowledge the fact that I draw heavily on the material Jane shares in her book in the next few chapters.

I love the way Jane puts it when she says "the simple fact is that you'll experience much more joy if you take control of the way, you approach life from the point of view of what goes on in your mind, rather than living totally mindlessly. You'll also experience more peace of mind, and improve your health, your relationships, and your prospects of a happy and healthy future." We really need to be on the ball in this regard because the world we live in could rightly be accused of judging women in general, and older women in particular, in relation to the kind of crazy reference points the quote from Einstein at the beginning of this chapter plays with. The upside is that the ball is in our court in terms of being in the position to decide how we respond to the plethora of cultural/emotional undercurrents that we're likely to experience in one way or another as we move through our lives.

The bottom line is that taking the time to look under the hood to see what's going on in your head on a day-to-day basis, will set you up to avoid wasting time on mindless thoughts and actions that can spiral out of control into unhappiness, self-sabotage, obsessions and even addictions. I've had a fair bit of experience with this kind of thing myself, and I'm going to bet that many of you have as well. What's important here is that I arrived at a number of strategies that are effective in bringing me back to my center whenever I stray. In fact, you'll find one of my all-time favorite resources called Yoga Nidra described in some detail at the end of this chapter.

The problem that's likely to come up sooner or later as we start to change anything substantial in our life, is that it's all too easy to default to the old patterns of thinking that got us to the place we need to move away from to be well. What we need to do is to establish new patterns that are going to get us to where we want to be, and deliberately revert back to them if we ever veer off track. If you think about the fact that we've been wiring the old patterns into our brain for years or even decades, then it's not surprising to accept that there's a serious act of will required to reprogram ourselves for success in relation to our health, and any other goals we might have. That's what this book is all about.

For example, Jane talks very openly these days about the way a deep sense of being 'broken' resulted in her developing a dysfunctional relationship with food. This played out as a forty-year history of Binge Eating Disorder for her. And for my own part, I can attest to the fact that the early and continuous programming I was exposed to through the church, the dance world and my schooling, led me to believe that I was not good enough in general, and that in particular I was a sinner who deserved whatever difficulties life threw at me. One of the many consequences of this limiting belief was that a solid sense of self-worth was non-existent for me for a very long time. One of the ways this played out was through a chronic tendency to compare my results unfavorably with the results I thought others working in the fitness industry were getting. Fairly regularly I would wind up feeling an almost overwhelming level of resentment about the fact that people I regarded as being less well credentialed than I was were getting opportunities that I was missing out on.

What I can say now after several decades of working with people from all walks of life in my wellness business, is that most of us to some degree or other have issues around worthiness. You don't have to look too far to see there's an epidemic of 'not good enough' thinking going on out there. As Brené Brown says in her great book *Daring Greatly*, "after all of the consciousness raising and critical awareness, we still feel the most shame about not being thin, young, and beautiful enough."

Brené Brown is renowned for her work on shame and vulnerability. Once we delve below the surface level of our life, it's not too hard to see the kind of damage we do to ourselves when we sit in shame. Not to mention the fact that avoiding vulnerability leads to the adoption of all kinds of unhelpful and unhealthy behaviors that stop us from seeing all the ways in which we are good enough. The questions I ask you to consider throughout the chapters in this book are aimed at helping you to be able to recognize and stare down any negative beliefs you've picked up in the process of becoming the woman you are today.

As Jane says, "being a woman is kind of like being the proverbial square peg trying to fit in a round hole that's been shaped by the artificial image of women we see reflected on magazine covers, in the movies, and in advertisements for clothes, beauty products and any commodities that are associated with being successful." We're also all too familiar with the sensationalized photos of celebrities who've put on weight, or who dare to set foot outside without their make up on, or those who've been dumped by their celebrity husband for a younger version of themself.

These things subtly reinforce our more or less entrenched and probably unconscious inferiority complexes, and function to shame us into a level of submission that is driven by toxic 'not good enough' thinking. Of course, the logical part of our brain knows that the images of perfection we see in magazines and on social media channels like Instagram are usually manipulated with the help of Photoshop and phone apps, not to mention the plethora of cosmetic procedures available to women to get closer to the image of 'beauty' that we're unconsciously measuring ourselves against.

The frustrating thing is that the logical part of our brain is usually overshadowed by the emotional part. That's why we're still vulnerable to the corrosive effects these images have on our sense of self-worth. If this isn't summed up by Einstein's idea of a fish feeling bad about itself because it can't ride a bicycle, then I don't know what is.

Women like Jane and I have spent the best part of our life being distracted by concerns about how much we weigh, how we look, and how much body fat we have when we compare ourselves to the probably photoshopped images of female icons that are featured not only in magazines, but also across the range of screen-based media including Facebook and Instagram that we are expose to on a daily basis.

Both of us run businesses that rely on our profiles being high, therefore withdrawing from these platforms is not an option for us. Basically, I'm baring my soul here so that you can see you are not alone if you're struggling with body image issues yourself. What I want you to know is that feelings of inferiority do not spring naturally out of being a woman. What they spring out of is the thousand and one sensory inputs we're exposed to as we grow up and move through our life.

At this juncture, a great reality check and self-care strategy that you might like to indulge in is to look at Celeste Barber's Instagram account. Both she and Taryn Brumfit (who is the brains behind the *Embrace Movement*), are pioneers in levelling the playing field for women like us.

MINDSET HABITS TO AVOID:

There are three mindset habits that Jane writes about in her book that I want to bring your attention to here. These are blame, justification, and denial. I've heard some great examples of these from clients of mine who neglect their wellbeing by always putting their own needs last, with reasons like:

- I'm a mum and it's my job to put others first.
- It's natural for my body to feel stiff and achy because I'm not a young woman anymore.
- I am as tired as I am because I'm responsible for the whole family, and with everything I must do on a daily basis, I simply don't have any time left to exercise.
- I can't bear the shame I'll feel at the gym because I will look 'too old' and 'too fat' with all those young people in their trendy activewear at the gym.
- I don't fit in, and I can't find a class time to suit me.

These kinds of things keep us stuck because they make it possible for us to believe our lack of progress toward our health goals can be explained by something other than our failure to take responsibility for our own wellbeing. In addition to the ideas around blame, justification, and denial I've already mentioned, there are also things like generalising and perfectionism that can keep us cycling around our problems without making any progress toward overcoming them.

I love the way Brené Brown puts things. She describes perfectionism as being nothing more than a case of shame wearing a disguise that ultimately keeps us small. She also explains that 'not good enough' thinking is the language of shame that leaves us feeling as if there's something horribly wrong with us at our core. Generalising takes the idea that 'I'm not good enough' and turns it into 'I'll never be good enough' or 'I'm no good at anything'.

My mission is to help as many women as I can to take their power back. That includes you, and it starts with catching yourself whenever you notice yourself defaulting to perfectionistic thinking, or generalising, or resorting to blame, justification, or denial. If you notice any of these things happening, I want you to deliberately rewrite the script you're playing out in your mind. This can be both painful and incredibly freeing at the same time. What it's all about is training yourself to be mindful of negative self-talk that can spring up at any time, and turn it around into a more empowering narrative. Doing this repeatedly will rewire your brain and eventually establish much more positive patterns of thinking.

You'll be hearing more about the importance of being mindful of the way your relationships impact the quality of your day-to-day existence soon. So with this in mind, I want you to answer the questions below as honestly as you can. This is my way of inviting you to pause for a moment and reflect on how you're positioned in relation to self-care in general, and in relation to having a supportive mindset in place.

- Are there any people in your life that you always come away from interacting with feeling bad in general, and/or about yourself in particular?
- If so, do you have healthy boundaries with these people?
    - If not, when are you going to establish them?
    - If you need help with this, when are you going to seek it?
- Where are you applying perfectionism in your life?
- How do you feel about that aspect of your life right now?
- In what ways are you doing well in this aspect of your life?
- In which other areas of your life are you doing well?
- What drains your energy?
    - What could you do to limit this drainage?
- How do you show yourself respect?
    - How else could you show yourself respect?
- How easy or hard have you made it to feel good about yourself?
- What could you do to make it easier to feel good about yourself?
- When do you numb yourself?
- How and Why do you numb yourself?
- What has numbing yourself cost you so far in your life?
- What could you replace this behavior with?
- What do you say to yourself when you've made a mistake?
    - What's a more empowering thing you could say?
- What do you say to yourself when you see your reflection in the mirror?
    - What's a more compassionate and empowering thing you could say?
- What do you say to yourself when you're tired?
    - What's a more compassionate thing you could say?
- What things could you do to cultivate more self-compassion?

To reward you for doing the work involved in answering these questions, and taking on board the need to make a commitment to self-care, I'm going to share one of the best ways I know to get grounded and reconnect to our inner self in the incredibly busy world we all live in. The tool I'm sharing with you here is called Yoga Nidra.

YOGA NIDRA:

Yoga Nidra is often described as the waking sleep. If you're able to go with the process without overthinking it, the practice of Yoga Nidra will enable you to get into a state of complete physical, emotional, and mental relaxation. You might feel like you're sleeping, but in fact what's happening is the unconscious part of your mind is functioning at a much deeper level than you're used to. The incredibly positive benefits of establishing a regular Yoga Nidra practise include stress reduction, improved productivity, better quality sleep, relief from anxiety and depression, and increased wellbeing overall.

Before you read the instructions below, I'd like you to go to Bodyandbalance.com.au and download the Yoga Nidra backing track that I'm making available to you to enhance your experience of this wonderful practice.

To start Yoga Nidra, you lie on your back with your arms away from your body and your palms turned upwards. This pose is called Shavasana or the Corpse Pose.

Your feet should be approximately hip width apart with your toes falling outwards. It's ideal to keep your eyes closed throughout the practice. You might also like to place a lavender pillow over your eyes to enhance the experience.

It's best if your body is symmetrical while you're lying on the floor. A good way to achieve this is to imagine a centre line running from the soles of your feet to the crown of your head. This position is said to promote a balance in the flow of life force throughout the body known as Chi.

When I teach Yoga Nidra, I include an intention setting exercise to help my clients establish a resolve around something they want to achieve. The exact words I use when I'm running a session, are "See it. Say it to yourself. Feel what it is like. Make it happen, and release it to the Universe." I'd like to invite you to repeat these words several times silently to yourself as you're relaxing. After this, as you listen to the recording, I'll be instructing you to individually and purposely relax the muscles in the main parts of your body, one at a time.

As far as setting your intention before starting the Yoga Nidra goes, it could be something as simple as wanting more love in your life. Or it could be about being kinder to yourself. Or it could be something very specific like getting a new job or giving up smoking. The other thing you'll notice I do within the Yoga Nidra session is guide you to focus on your breath before and after the deep relaxation phase. In fact, if you were to disregard everything else you read in this book, and only start focussing on your breath regularly throughout the day, you will still be streets ahead in terms of your health, especially if you are anything like the millions of people out there who are living a life full of way too much stress, and way too little rest and relaxation.

Don't worry if you've tried this kind of thing before, and for whatever reason it hasn't 'worked' for you. I also sometimes find that resistance and frustration will bubble up when I'm trying to get into the 'right' space. One of the reasons this happens is that we all have what's often called the 'monkey mind'. Monkey mind is the term that's used to describe the constant passing of thoughts that clutter our mind and ultimately exhaust us mentally, physically, and emotionally. Beyond just exhausting us though, monkey mind can be even more unhelpful by distracting us from what's important. That said, if you turn your focus inward and really listen to what's going on under the monkey mind, there might be an important message for you there.

For example as I mentioned earlier, I was following a voice that was guiding me into a meditative state recently. And when the word 'soul' was spoken it triggered my monkey mind to go into overdrive. This resulted in what at first just seemed like an incredibly unsettling bunch of random thoughts. But they eventually condensed into an insight that helped me to see the extent to which my life had been shaped by my early experiences. That's why I delve into the question of the societal influences that are bearing down on us in the next chapter.

I want to conclude this chapter with a piece of feedback I received from a client who has been working with me for over 19 years. Her name is Margaret Campbell. She said that "When I wake up at 4:00am or thereabouts every night, what I hear is your voice saying relax like you do in the Yoga Nidra sessions Jill. That always puts me straight back to sleep." I really hope you get a positive outcome like Margaret regularly does when you download your Yoga Nidra recording and give this simple but incredibly powerful practice a go.

CHAPTER THREE

THE WORLD WE LIVE IN

As well as instilling a passion for movement and dance in me, the fact that I was involved in the ballet world from a very early age made me hyper-vigilant about my weight. While I can accept the fact that body weight and shape have an impact on our ability to do particular kinds of movements, what I don't find acceptable is the dance world's all but total exclusion of anyone who isn't super slim. I want to acknowledge that some dance companies in the 21st Century appear to appreciate the value of a fit and toned body over a super skinny one, but these companies are well and truly in the minority.

I know firsthand that the pressure to be skinny is still alive and well in the world of classical ballet. For example, a girl from my local community was thrilled to be accepted into a prestigious dance company in Europe a few years ago. She was 15 at the time and worked incredibly hard to adhere to the company's archaic requirement to keep her weight below 47kg. You don't need a medical degree to know that 47kg is nowhere near a healthy weight for an above average height 15-year-old girl like the one in question. This wonderful young woman was putting her health at risk by limiting the calories she was taking into her body for fear of being kicked out of the company.

Finding out about this young woman's story reminded me of an issue that emerged during Australian Fashion Week a few years ago. In this case it was the celebrated 'anorexic' look of the models in one of the shows that inspired an uproar among (what some 'traditionalists' were inclined to call) an increasingly loud and influential 'politically correct' group of health professionals and others. One of the models involved in this show was a friend of my daughter. I know for a fact that she suffered greatly from the lack of nutrients that were going into her body over the sustained period of time she worked in the fashion industry. Fortunately, this inspirational woman was able to come out the other side and is now gaining traction as she advocates for change through sharing her story.

You can hear her talking about her experiences here - www.huffingtonpost.com.au/2016/11/06/dying-to-be-a-model-the-torment-of-an-eating-disorder-and-life_a_21599936/

It really breaks my heart to think about the baggage we load ourselves up with by virtue of the images we see in magazines and on the screens that reflect an artificial ideal that only a very few people could ever achieve. The cold hard fact is that this makes most girls and women feel inadequate, and that places us at risk of hating our own fabulous healthy bodies.

I've had to fight my own demons in this regard. I've gone way too far with restricting calories, and spending way too much time thinking about what I can and can't eat because of the belief I had about my body needing to be 'perfect' before I could feel worthy. These days I'm grateful to be able to say that I've settled into a more healthy and comfortable relationship with my body, and the food that I put into it. That relationship is based around a moderate approach to intermittent fasting. This approach allows me to eat the foods that I love in the knowledge that I am doing great things for my body.

This way of maintaining a healthy weight, and in the process ageing well, was popularised in 2015 by Michael Mosley with his best-selling book *The 5/2 Diet*. The approach can be summed up by saying that eating 'normally' for 5 days, and restricting calories to 500 per day for 2 days each week, enables people to lose body fat and keep it off over the long term. I don't follow the 5/2 approach myself. What I do instead is replace some of my meals with high nutrition shakes with a base of high-quality protein from peas and brown rice. I devised the recipe I use through trial and error over a period of years. You'll find it on my website at www.bodyandbalance.com.au if you'd like to try it out. This approach to my diet works well for me because it keeps my weight within a healthy and comfortable range, as well as giving me plenty of energy to maintain a schedule that includes running 1or 2 exercise classes a day, 6 days a week.

I'm in a great place now, but I've had problems with my body image for most of my life. I can see that the rot was set well before adolescence, but the way I felt about my body took a turn for the worse when I was about 12 and my shape started to change. The day my mother told me that my ballet teacher had counselled her about cutting back on my food was a pivotal moment in my life. The goal was (among other things) for me to stop menstruating.

Knowing what I know now about how the body works, I'm appalled that this was the kind of advice mothers like mine were not only given, but also prepared to follow. I'm especially appalled because of the dreadful effect it had on my peace of mind, as well as my behaviour around food. All I can do is shake my head when I think about how much of my life was spent believing that I was too fat when I was younger, when I only have to look at photos of myself to see that if anything, I was probably too thin.

The saying that old habits die hard rings true here. I say that because I occasionally catch myself in an unguarded moment verging into problematic territory around my body image. I see this as a terrible legacy of the environment I grew up in, and still live in for that matter. It amazes me that this can be so, because I have a high level of awareness around the dangers of restricting calories at the expense of nourishing our body with the nutrition it needs to be well.

Looking back over everything I've gone through to get to where I am now, I must remind myself to practice self-compassion as I reflect on the fact that I've lived with body image issues for almost all my life. And I'm prepared to publicly declare that this is where it stops - right here and right now. Because now is the time to turn our back on all the external pressures to be thin, and open the gate to freedom for ourselves and our children, whether they've been born yet or not.

What I want to urge you to do is pay attention to loved ones if they tell you they're worried about the amount of weight you're losing. Because if you're heading into (or worse still, if you're already deep in) the throws of anorexia, you will have lost your ability to honestly assess whether you've taken the idea of wanting to lose a bit of weight too far. Frankly, if people are noticing that you're shrinking, then it's very likely that you have taken things too far. I say that because the earliest warning signs of anorexia can be very difficult to distinguish from the behaviour of people on 'normal' weight loss diets. Not to mention the fact that because there is so much at stake for people with anorexia to avoid putting on weight, they're likely to become incredibly resourceful when it comes to concealing their behaviour around food.

There's no totally straightforward path when it comes to recovering from an eating disorder. What I find interesting is that some people have found lifting weights to be beneficial as they work toward recovery. It appears that focussing on their body in a way that values feeling strong rather than being thin, helps people to redefine their relationship with themselves. The key here is to refocus women on what they can do to feel good in their body, rather than staying stuck in the trap of paying way too much attention to the question of how they look.

On a cautionary note, I want to throw in the fact that swapping one obsession for another is not what recovery looks like. I say this because overexercising is a problem in its own right. At the end of the day, as Amanda Schlitzer who is the strength and conditioning coach who runs a program called the *Victory Challenge* in New York City says, "It's all about making sure your mindset is in the right place... Sometimes people will switch over to exercising after an eating disorder and be extremely rigid with their fitness routine. But it's important to embrace mental flexibility and take rest days, add in variety, and be flexible if things come up. You need to be in the right mindset to trust your intentions, listen to your body, and modify what you are doing if needed."

Before I move on, I want to say that if you think you might be suffering from an eating disorder of any kind, the first step is to reach out for help. There are organisations all over the world that will support you. The Butterfly Foundation is a national support organisation in Australia where I'm based. Their helpline is 1800334673 and their website is thebutterflyfoundation.org.au. A Google search will point you to the relevant organisation in whatever part of the world you are in.

Notwithstanding the scrutiny we put ourselves under, the other pressure women are under is the way our bodies are objectified by the gaze and behaviour of some of the men we are likely to encounter. My reading of the #MeToo movement is that we've come to a tipping point where the message that we are not prepared to take it anymore is starting to really hit home.

Essentially what the American actress Alyssa Milano did in 2017 was dramatically raise awareness of the physical, mental and verbal abuse that is commonplace for females in all sorts of contexts, ranging from those working in the entertainment and arts industries, to those working in the political sphere. The #MeToo movement opened a flood of previously hidden stories that have flushed out the double bind that women are in when they are consumed with shame, rather than the white-hot fury they're entitled to feel when abuse is perpetrated against them.

The public discourse around the #MeToo movement that outed high profile men like Harvey Weinstein and Geoffrey Epstein who had been abusing literally 100's of women, has been somewhat overshadowed by the Pandemic and the rebuilding of democracy in America in the post-Trump era. But we all know that there's still a lot more work to be done when it comes to what we might loosely call 'equality'.

Of course, there is a lot more to equality than stopping women being physically and emotionally abused by men. I'm not going to delve into the question of the lack of gender equality when it comes to pay rates and access to opportunities in the workplace. What I will say though is that writing about this material brought up a lot of anger I had been repressing without even knowing it. Like many other women, I've also been a victim of extreme sexism and harassment. These experiences violated not only my body, but my psyche as well. When I really thought about it, it was like being abused again via the disempowerment I felt when it came to speaking out about some of the things that happened to me when I was a young girl. Rather than dredging it all up here, I want to share what I came up with when I thought about what I would say to my eight-year-old self if she was here with me now. What came up was:

"You are strong even if it sometimes feels like you aren't.
You have not done anything wrong.
You do not deserve this. You are not a victim.
You can do anything you put your mind to.
And you will grow up to be a strong and powerful woman
who doesn't beat herself up for not being perfect."

I'd love for you to experience how wonderful it feels to write something like I just wrote for yourself. So, let me ask you - what would you say to your eight-year-old self if she was sitting next to you now?

You'll recall I shared my experience as an eight-year-old girl walking through Hyde Park in Sydney to get to my ballet classes earlier. As I reflect on that time, it makes me feel sick when I think about the fear I felt as a little girl who had to run for her life from the sleazy men who were hanging around the park, just to get to the ballet school unscathed. Although when I think about it, I wasn't unscathed, because I'm wearing the psychological scars of that period just as surely as I would be wearing the physical scars if I wasn't able to run as fast as I did back then.

What's more, it makes me sad to reflect on the fact that my ability to run didn't do me any good when it came to my father's drunk male friends who unashamedly groped me in the back seat of the car on the way home from ballet. In fact, I was shocked when I realised the inevitability of being violated was so inculcated in my psyche, that I accepted that this was just the way things were back then. I guess my preparedness to accept being groped in the back of my father's car is not so surprising in the context of the disgraceful behaviour of priests and nuns in the Catholic school system that I was educated within.

#MeToo has given me the audacity to hope there's a future not too far away where it would be inconceivable for any 'normal' man (by that I mean anyone who is not a sociopath or psychopath) to abuse and/or debase women in any way. The sad thing is that I carry the legacy of a deep distrust of men around with me to this day. That said, I'm filled with gratitude to be married to a truly wonderful and totally trustworthy man who has created a very different legacy for our daughter Elodie. From her perspective, by far the majority of the male population are very decent people. I've only told her about a few stories from my past because I walk a fine line between not making her overly fearful, and wanting her to appreciate the importance of being wary because terrible things can and do happen to ordinary young women just like her.

Sadly enough, my daughter Elodie was inspired to write a post on Facebook about feeling uncomfortable when she was performing in a Sydney club as a singer recently. Her discomfort related to the fact that a not insignificant proportion of the audience seemed to think it was ok to stare at her breasts and/or crotch while she was singing. This experience was echoed by other female singers she spoke to and confirms that we still have some way to go. I say that because these young women not only felt powerless in the gaze of these leering men, but they also felt like they were at risk of losing the income they got from performing if they spoke out about the way the behaviour of some of the male patrons made them feel.

Hearing about this really brought it all back for me when I realised the age of the men in question meant that they could be contemporaries of the boys who harassed me for simply being an outspoken female walking to the beat of her own drum when I was young. It still really troubles me that I was targeted because I was inclined to dress 'differently'. And believe me I paid dearly for having the audacity to dress the way I wanted to because on one particular occasion I was attacked viciously by a group of Sydney footballers who told me I looked like a slut.

I still carry baggage as a result of that incident, including the fact that the girls who saved me from the attack told me they were always careful not to wear anything that was likely to provoke the boys on account of rape being so common in the Northern Beaches of Sydney where we all lived at the time. In other words, these girls saw no other way to keep themselves safe than to stifle their freedom and creativity.

I believe these kinds of attitudes still exist in some form or other. For example, I was told by a well-known sportsperson not so long ago that he felt the only way to protect his girlfriend from his teammates was to make sure she stayed away from them until well after the game had finished. What he was getting at was that coupled with their sense of 'entitlement', the testosterone levels in the bodies of the football players meant that his girlfriend would be unsafe in their presence. What a shocking indictment is that?

As I said earlier though, the #MeToo movement has given me hope of a brighter future.

Something else that has given me hope is an ever so slight watering down of agism which is another one of the secret killers of women's self-esteem that I have on my radar. One of the signs of agism being watered down came in the form of being asked to pose for photographs to appear in a book called *This is Me #unretouched*. This book is full of portraits of women and their journeys to self-love and acceptance. It was pulled together by Julia Adams and Gergie Abay. The portraits feature women of all ages telling their story wearing only a swimsuit, and no make-up. The idea was to keep our stories and our appearance raw and real. As Julia and Gergie said, "Working on this book has been a powerful insight into the hearts of women all over the world. Through my own experience I've learned that no-one is immune from self-love issues ... I hope you [can now] look in the mirror with self-acceptance and love."

CHAPTER FOUR

THE BODY WE LIVE IN

We are going right back to the fundamentals of how the body works here so that you can see why it's worth putting the time into aligning what you think, eat, and do with the goal of being well.

Going back to fundamentals includes getting a basic level of understanding about:

- The role of hormones.
- The body's processes for getting energy from food.
- The body's processes for eliminating waste.
- The effects of stress, diet, exercise, and mindset on all of the above.

An overarching principle in all of this is that the body's processes are aimed at achieving homeostasis. Homeostasis is the word used to describe internal stability. The rationale for the recommendations in this book is based on the fact that not turning around poor lifestyle habits will result in your body being forced to work harder than it should to maintain the degree of homeostasis it needs to function well.

We all know people who smoke, drink excessively, and eat copious amounts of sugar-laden processed foods, yet never seem to get sick. What I want to say is that these kinds of behaviors might work ok when we're young, and the signs of the toll they're taking on our body might not show up for a very long time, but believe me they will show up. And I promise you it's not going to be pretty when they do.

My plan is to help you to get an understanding of what goes on in your body by taking a look at what goes on within our cells. We're starting here because cells are the fundamental building blocks of the body. Specifically, it's the way cells access energy that sheds light on how much control we have around the way we feel, look, and age.

The tube-like structures within cells called mitochondria are particularly important. It's mitochondria that is responsible for generating most of the body's energy. Oxygen is critical to the process of generating energy because it helps metabolise the nutrients released from the food we eat during digestion. Oxidation results from combining oxygen with other elements, so this process of releasing energy is a double-edged sword. I say that because while the body needs oxygen to survive, oxidation damages cell membranes and other structures that are vital to our ongoing health.

Meanwhile the free radicals that oxidants produce are critical to our health. Free radicals are great because they help to kill invading bacteria as part of the immune system. They tend to get a bit of a bad rap in the way vitamin supplements and the like are advertised though. But it turns out that they're critical to our body's ability to fight off disease. It's only when we have more free radicals than our body can handle that we're going to have a problem.

A free radical is an atom with at least one unpaired electron in its outer cell. Atoms need a pair of electrons to be stable. If two electrons aren't present, the atom will go searching for another electron it can steal to correct the situation. The only problem is that losing an electron causes the other molecule to become unstable.

The situation with free radicals is a great example of the way the body brings about homeostasis. It also sheds light on what can happen when the systems in our body are stressed by an unhealthy lifestyle that results in an oversupply of free radicals. When the conditions are right though, the body releases naturally occurring antioxidants after the oxidants have done their job. Antioxidants (which are either produced by our bodies or taken in when we eat the right kinds of foods) are thought to prevent some of the damage done by free radicals by neutralizing them with a spare electron that pairs with the single one. Antioxidants are the only molecules that don't become unstable when they lose an electron. That's why it's important to maintain a diet that delivers an adequate supply of antioxidants on a daily basis.

The problem with free radicals is that the body is damaged when unstable molecules float around looking for another electron to pair with. If the molecule was part of a cell wall for example, the wall will be damaged as the molecule separates from it in search of another electron. A big problem here is that the part of the cell that's most likely to be attacked when the cell wall is damaged is the DNA. This matters because the genetic information in our DNA is the code that runs every process in our body.

As well as being produced naturally by the body's own processes, free radicals also result from the environments we live in. Things like poor air quality, fast food, chemicals, preservatives, smoking, drinking to excess, and stress, contribute to the free radical load present in our body at any given time. So, if our lifestyle results in the balance of oxidants and antioxidants being disturbed to the extent that our DNA is damaged, over time we'll be at risk of not only experiencing health problems, but also speeding up the aging process.

The good news is that the ball is in our court because we can easily fill our diet with antioxidant rich foods including fruits like blueberries, pomegranates and apples, as well as a wide range of vegetables and nuts. There are also a number of good quality multivitamins on the market that contain vitamin A, vitamin C, vitamin E and selenium. These are the vitamins that boost the level of antioxidants in the body.

The state of our digestive system is absolutely central to the way we absorb food. When I ask my clients what they know about their digestive system, they often miss out on the critical first step. That is chewing. You might have been told that you need to chew each bite of food 32 times before swallowing it when you were growing up (I know

I was). But do you actually do it? Not many people do. In fact, it isn't a very accurate instruction anyway, because obviously you need to chew a bite you've taken out of a piece of steak a lot more than you need to chew a grape for example. The point is that you want to make sure you chew your food enough for it to be digested well.

After it is chewed and swallowed, the food we eat makes its way into our stomach where it's mixed with the acids and enzymes that get it ready to be digested. This involves the carbohydrate being broken down into glucose to be released into the bloodstream where it's available to be used for energy immediately or stored away for use later. Insulin is critical to this process. That's why a lack of insulin or insulin resistance is such a big problem.

A particularly worrying trend that's been building since processed foods came into the picture in the 1950s is that increasing numbers of people are being diagnosed with diabetes. Diabetes comes about either as a result of the body halting or slowing down the production of insulin or developing resistance to it. Approximately 280 Australians develop diabetes every day, with almost 1.1 million currently living with diagnosed diabetes.

When everything is working well though, insulin is released from the pancreas when it's required, and transported through the bloodstream sending a signal to the cells to let the glucose in. Blood sugar levels start to drop as glucose moves from the bloodstream into the cells. This then sends a signal to the pancreas to reduce the amount of insulin it's releasing. This results in the amount of glucose going into the cells decreasing. This balancing act happens many times throughout the day as energy is either being used or stored.

There are a couple of important things to take into account here. The first one is that our ability to control our blood sugar levels decreases as we age. The other one is that we start producing more advanced glycation end products known as AGEs as we get older. AGEs are harmful byproducts of the process the body uses to make energy from glucose. The problem with AGEs is that they attach to and damage the proteins in our skin and arteries. This causes them to become stiffer and less effective. That means AGEs not only contribute to things that we can see like our skin wrinkling, but they also predispose us to more serious problems like cardiovascular disease through the hardening of our arteries.

As mentioned above, AGEs are made in small quantities as a byproduct of the body's process of metabolizing sugar. The problem is that our body becomes overloaded with them when we eat a lot of processed foods in particular. This is because the processing methods that make these foods digestible and storable raises AGEs to a level that is not good for our body. The problem is that our body responds to AGEs like it responds to an infection with a low level of inflammation arising out of the process.

The bottom line is that a diet that results in AGEs building up in the body to the extent that they cause excessive oxidation and inflammation will slowly but surely damage our organs and speed up the aging process. Prolonged elevated levels of AGEs are linked with conditions like heart disease, stroke, arthritis, kidney disease and dementia. The good news is that staying away from processed foods that load the body with AGEs will help you to avoid unnecessary levels of inflammation that puts stress on the body.

HORMONES:

What we're going to do now is look at the role hormones play in all of this. Hormones are chemical substances made by our organs to control the different processes that take place within the body. That's why hormones are often referred to as chemical messengers. As we've seen earlier, insulin for example is a hormone made by the pancreas to regulate the amount of glucose in the blood. A couple of other interesting hormones involved in the digestive process are ghrelin and leptin. Ghrelin is the hormone that stimulates appetite, while leptin is the one that tells us when we're full.

Even though hormones control almost every process that keeps our body alive, we are unlikely to give them much thought until something goes wrong. An example of something that can go wrong for women is a condition called endometriosis. About one in ten women experience endometriosis which is a condition where the tissue that is meant to line the uterus grows outside of it and attaches to other areas where it doesn't belong. This is an incredibly painful condition that often results in women opting for a hysterectomy. That's certainly not a great option for women who are keen to have children. Fortunately, relief from the pain of endometriosis has been known to result from alternative therapies like acupuncture, chiropractic care, ingesting herbs like cinnamon twig or liquorice root, and using supplements such as thiamine (vitamin B1), magnesium, or omega-3 fatty acids.

Hormones also make their way to the top of our mind when we start to go through a life stage like menopause. The two main hormones made by the ovaries to bring menopause about are progesterone and estrogen. Perimenopause is the stage before menopause where the ovaries start to make less estrogen. It can begin as early as the 30s in some women, but it's more likely to kick in during the mid to late 40s. It tends to be in the latter stages of perimenopause when we're likely to start noticing symptoms that can include things like irregular periods, hot flushes, irregular heartbeat, mood swings, anxiety, sleep problems, loss of libido, vaginal dryness, fatigue, lack of mental clarity, incontinence, aching joints and muscles, and unexplained weight gain.

None of this is inevitable though, and being in great health when your hormones start to shift will stand you in good stead to move through menopause well, especially if you don't let your mindset undermine you. Now that you've got tools like Yoga Nidra and the other material I shared in the self-care chapter in your toolbox, as well as the other things I'm sharing in the following chapters, you'll be well positioned to pivot your way through a life phase that has the potential to stymie less well-prepared people.

Menopause takes over from perimenopause 12 months after menstruation ceases. It is usually established somewhere between the ages of 45 and 54, although it can start earlier and finish later than that. The whole period can last up to 10 years, after which the symptoms will wear off. While that is great news for anyone who is struggling with some or all the symptoms listed above, there is a downside to the cessation of menopause. The downside is that we are predisposed to an increased risk of a number of conditions such as osteoporosis and heart disease in the post-menopause phase. This is where the question of hormone replacement therapy (HRT) often arises.

The thing about hormones is that they are all about balance. It's the interruption to the normal balance of estrogen and progesterone that brings about the changes we experience when we're dealing with conditions like endometriosis and menopause. Many women suffer with intense period pain thinking that it's normal, and others suffer with intense hot flushes thinking it is normal. But these things are the symptoms of hormonal imbalances.

All I can do is shake my head when I think about having been put on the birth control pill as a 15-year-old because I had severe period pain and heavy loss of blood that resulted in anemia. While I was grateful for the pill because it helped me cope with my periods, I now realise I was probably suffering from endometriosis that went undiagnosed and untreated.

These kinds of things happen because of the assumptions doctors make in the interest of getting people like me out of their office as quickly as they can. I don't know what it's like in your part of the world, but in Australia where I live doctors work to strict schedules where they're unlikely to pick up on anything but the most obvious reasons for the conditions their patients are showing up with. Although I was able to have a child, I discovered that my tubes were blocked with the characteristic scar tissue of endometriosis. And because of this, having my second child was like being on a long and very emotional roller coaster.

When I started to have symptoms of menopause, I didn't give synthetic hormones a moments thought because I turned to alternative approaches such as exercise, bio-identical hormones, and changes to my diet. This worked for me, but many women choose synthetic HRT for relief. To my mind, if you find yourself struggling with the symptoms you're experiencing and you're interested in investigating HRT or other options, the best idea is to have your hormone levels checked by your doctor and decide what to do once you know exactly what you're dealing with.

As far as I'm concerned, adjusting your lifestyle in relation to exercise, nutrition, stress management and the quality of the sleep you're getting is the best place to start. In other words, I wouldn't be jumping straight in and taking HRT before exploring other less invasive options first.

This question of HRT is a reasonably controversial one. Back in the days when the mothers of people like Jane and myself went into menopause, synthetic hormone replacement therapy was thought to be completely safe. What's more, it was widely regarded to be the only way to go in terms of managing the symptoms of menopause. Similarly, now days the pill is prescribed without hesitation for birth control and period-related issues without regard for the consequences of fooling around with the natural ebb and flow of hormones in a young woman's body.

I'd have hoped that the care people take when deciding what to put into their bodies would have evolved since my mother's time, but that seems not to be the case. Things actually seemed to get worse as the medical establishment experimented with new and not fully tested vaccines in a strategy to control the Covid Pandemic. I saw many cases of vaccine-driven physical and mental responses that were anything but positive when I was a teacher of children with disabilities back in the 1990's. I know we've had amazing results with the eradication of things like polio through vaccination, but we are yet to see what our future looks like in an even more heavily vaccinated world.

My mother didn't take HRT because menopause wasn't a big deal for her, but she did take the popular analgesics like Bex and APC powders for the intense migraines she suffered. Even though there's no doubt these drugs posed a threat to her liver, I don't begrudge her for using them, because the quality of her life would have been terrible without them. Fortunately, her headaches decreased once she got past menopause.

Unfortunately, as I understand it many women have paid the price of taking the original forms of synthetic HRT by contracting breast cancer. Fortunately, there have been significant refinements over the last 50 years. What's more, taking synthetic HRT or just grinning and bearing the symptoms of menopause are no longer the only options available. bioidentical hormones, herbal remedies, and lifestyle management offer very effective alternative approaches to consider.

As you would know by now, I'm committed to helping women to take their power back. And as I see it, the best way for this to happen is by staying informed about what's going on inside our body, and critically assessing the pros and cons of the various options that are available to keep our body healthy at any given time.

CHAPTER FIVE

THE FOOD WE EAT

My aim in this chapter is to give you the information you need to be able to make healthy informed decisions about the food you put into your body.

The matter of what to eat is not only tricky because of the changing advice we get from the so-called experts, but also because of the way the diet industry has hijacked the agenda. A scan of the posts on Facebook and Instagram, not to mention the images on magazine covers, and the inboxes full of advice telling us to detox, shred fat, get bikini body ready for summer, or whatever the focus of the day might be, presents a dizzying array of options to consider. It's enough to drive a person crazy, especially at that trickiest of all times when young people are moving from childhood into womanhood. These are the people I worry about the most. They really have the odds stacked against them when it comes to maintaining a healthy level of self-esteem, and a realistic understanding of what their body needs in the way of nutrition to be well.

Of course, it's not only young girls who struggle in this regard. I have clients in their 50s and 60s who are pleasantly surprised when they find out how easy it is to support their body with sound nutrition. The multimillion-dollar diet industry would have us believe otherwise of course, but as far as I'm concerned, the 'secret' that I love to share is that all you need to do is approach life from the point of view of balance. You will never hear that kind of advice from the multinationals who make trillions of dollars off their ability to convince people like us that we need diet formulas, appetite suppressants, 7-day express programs for a flat belly, and God knows what else.

What I want you to know is that there is no need to cut out everything you love from your diet. I don't know your exact situation, but most people who come to me for help just need to switch things around a bit and consume more of the foods that support the processes going on in their body. To sum the situation up for you, what I want to say is that eating food is about providing our body with enough healthy carbohydrates, good quality protein, healthy fats, and an adequate amount of fibre, vitamins, minerals and water for hydration. I'm going to delve into the question of carbohydrates first, before looking at protein and the other components of nutrition in turn.

CARBOHYDRATES:

Carbohydrates are the essential fuel of the central nervous system. They are also the most efficient source of energy for the body. Carbohydrates should account for about half of our daily dietary intake, with as much of this as possible being in the complex form. Unfortunately, many of us have a history of filling our bodies up with way too many refined simple carbohydrates that lead to an increase in the level of sugar in our blood. Increasing blood sugar levels results in the release of insulin that helps to move the sugar from the blood to the cells where it can be used for energy. But excess blood sugar causes inflammation in the lining of the blood vessels, and can predispose our body to go into a state called syndrome X.

Syndrome X is the precursor to diabetes, so you need to avoid simple carbohydrates to increase your chances of avoiding Syndrome X. Simple carbohydrates are the ones found in processed foods like cakes, biscuits, breakfast cereals, and highly processed breads. On the other hand, the complex carbohydrates found in foods like oatmeal, rice, and some vegetables take much longer to digest. That means our blood sugar levels rise much more gradually than they do when we eat simple carbohydrates. The other problem with processed simple carbohydrates is that the changes they undergo during processing results in high levels of the damaging AGEs that you heard about earlier.

Gaining an understanding of the role glucose plays in transporting energy into the cells where it's used for fuel can be a turning point for people who have let themselves get out of the habit of eating well. The simple truth is that our bodies work much better on a diet of unrefined whole foods including carbohydrates from fruits, vegetables, and whole grains, rather than the unnaturally sweetened and flavoured processed foods that not only lead to spikes in sugar levels and inflammation in our body, but are also highly addictive, and can lead to cravings and over-consumption.

What this all means is that it's easier for our body to do what it needs to do when we adopt a wholefood approach, because among other things, loading our diet with whole foods avoids the repeated increases in blood sugar that causes unnecessary damage to the body. If you're someone who has unwittingly trained your body to crave the wrong kinds of food, this information will help you to be much more aware of what's at stake. I always say that knowledge is power, and my hope is that this knowledge will support you through what can initially be a very difficult process. And make no mistake about it. If your diet has tended to be overloaded with processed foods, then it will probably be difficult to kick this habit because refined sugar which is used in these foods is one of the most addictive substances in the world.

Some of you may be more familiar with deciding what food to eat with reference to the Glycaemic Index (GI). To simplify this somewhat more complicated system for working out what you should and shouldn't eat, you can focus on favouring foods that are known as low GI, and avoiding those that are known as high GI. Like simple carbohydrates, high GI foods break down quickly and result in spikes in blood sugar. Low GI foods on the other hand are broken down much more slowly and raise blood sugar levels much less, thus requiring less insulin to metabolize them. On a cautionary note, if you're using the GI approach to work out what to include in your diet, remember to favour foods that are as close to their natural state as possible. I say this because some of the foods that are ranked as low GI can still be laced with preservatives and artificial flavours and sweeteners that are just no good for the body.

FIBRE:

Another unfortunate effect of processing grains is that most of the fibre they contain naturally is lost. Fibre is incredibly important from the point of view of our overall health, not only because it keeps our bowel working well, but also because it helps reduce the level of bad cholesterol in our blood. It's also wonderful from the point of view of slowing down the rate of digestion so that much less insulin is released into our system, and we feel fuller for longer.

The sad fact is that too many people suffer from problems around the elimination of waste from their body because the processed foods they fill their diet with lack adequate levels of fibre. Sooner or later this way of eating is going to start causing problems because it is detrimental to the body's natural detoxification processes. If you find yourself getting a bit sluggish in this regard, the simple prescription is to include more fibre in your diet, to drink more water, and to do more exercise. If this doesn't work for you, it's worth seeking the help of a health professional sooner rather than later to see if you've got an underlying problem that needs to be addressed. It stands to reason that you're not going to be able to function at your best if the toxins created in the digestive process remain in your body longer than they should.

These days there's little doubt about the mind/body connection, but you might be surprised to learn just how much the health of our digestive system is interrelated with our emotional and psychological wellbeing. This is because 90% of the body's serotonin receptors are found within the gut. Serotonin is the neurotransmitter that's best known for its contribution to our ability to feel happy and well.

I find this very interesting in light of the levels of antidepressants being prescribed these days. It's been reported by the National Centre for Disease statistics in the USA that 13% of people in that country over the age of 12 take antidepressants. This statistic is slightly lower than the anecdotal evidence I have about the situation in Australia where I live. I wonder how different these statistics might be if more doctors started looking at what's going on in someone's gut when they present with depression before they get their prescription pad out to offer a pharmacological solution. I'm not suggesting there's no place for anti-depressants, but I'm wondering whether there might be equally if not more effective side-effect free options that aren't being fully explored.

I go deeper into the question of the importance of maintaining a healthy gut very soon. I do this because the impact the state of our gut has on our brain and our overall wellbeing is significant. But before we go there, I want to drive home the point that setting yourself up with a predominantly whole food, high fibre diet will not only lead to healthy levels of blood sugar and a healthier gut, but it will also keep your blood cholesterol low. We need some cholesterol to help maintain the health of our brain, skin, and other organs. The problem is that too many of us have unhealthy levels of low-density lipoprotein or LDL. This is a problem because LDL predisposes us to conditions like coronary artery disease and strokes.

Familial hypercholesterolemia is a disorder that is passed down through families. It causes LDL cholesterol levels to be very high. In some cases, the condition begins at birth and can cause heart attacks at an early age. In others, it's the food they eat that causes problems with cholesterol. In either case, diet is important. It's the LDL that we want to be lowering, because it carries the cholesterol away from the liver and into the bloodstream. LDL is the one that's involved in the build-up of plaque that can clog the arteries leading to an increased risk of heart attack or stroke. Whereas HDL on the other hand is known as the good cholesterol because it removes LDL from where it can do damage and transports it to the liver where it is broken down to be excreted.

FYI, because I have a genetic disposition toward high cholesterol myself, maintaining the approach to my diet that I mentioned earlier, along with the amount of exercise I do daily, keeps my cholesterol levels within a healthy range. What this means is that I don't need to take drugs like statins to keep my cholesterol in check.

FATS:

Fats are the most energy dense of the food groups. They are important because they support cell growth, and they are involved in the development and functioning of the brain. Fats are also critical to the production of many of our regulatory hormones. A healthy diet from the point of view of cholesterol includes eliminating saturated and trans fats (which are found in baked goods like cookies and cakes, as well as fried foods like chips), while including healthy fats like olive oil. You should aim for your diet to be made up of no more than 25% fat, with less than 10% of that coming from the saturated varieties.

The problem with trans fats is that they lower the good HDL cholesterol and increase the bad LDL cholesterol. Polyunsaturated fats like omega 3 and omega 6 oils are the much healthier options because they help to reduce the risk of heart disease, and they are precursors to other substances involved in regulating blood pressure and the body's inflammatory response. This means they can offset some of the dangerous processes we are exposed to as we age. In particular, Omega 6 in moderation has been seen to ease some of the symptoms of menopause. The cautionary note here is that it's important not to overdo it with Omega 6.

A balanced diet should include the healthier polyunsaturated fats and monounsaturated fats that are found in foods like avocados, almonds, and cooking oils made from plants or seeds.

PROTEIN:

Protein is the other main food group we need to consider. Because our body can't produce protein which is central to our ability to build and repair tissue, we need to consume it in our diet. In addition to building and repairing tissue, protein is also important from the point of view of the health of our immune system.

Adult women who exercise less than 30 minutes per day should consume 46 grams of protein every day. Animal products such as meats, milk, fish, and eggs are rich sources of protein. Because the proteins we get from animals are major sources of cholesterol, it's worth making sure you balance things out by also consuming the protein found in plant sources. Non-animal sources of protein for you to consider include non-genetically modified soybeans, legumes, nut butters, and some grains such as wheat germ and quinoa. As far as consuming animal sources of protein goes, it's important to trim the fat off meat, and favour chicken and fish over red meat. It's also important to avoid the production of AGEs by slow cooking, stewing, or steaming your meat, rather than frying, grilling and barbequing it.

To summarise what we've covered so far, I want you to note that you'll be helping your body to be well if you follow a wholefood approach to eating, with everything that passes your lips being as close to its natural state as possible. The body thrives on a diet that is mostly plant based, with the fruit and vegetable foundation being augmented by unprocessed complex carbohydrates, healthy fats, protein, fibre, vitamins, minerals, and water for hydration. You'll be minimizing the damage free radicals do by including a wide range of foods that supply an adequate amount and range of antioxidants.

It's not a pretty picture when I look back over the history of diet fads, some of which I fell prey to myself. If your background is anything like mine, you could probably chart the history of diets over the last 50 or so years by looking at your bookcase. If I was to line my books up chronologically, I'd have a couple focussed on the low-fat approaches to eating, followed by the low carbohydrate approaches, then the Paleo-type high protein approaches, and of course a couple focussing on intermittent fasting.

Then there are approaches that focus on getting your body into a state called autophagy. This literally means that the body is eating itself. The more extreme approaches to achieving this state involve complete deprivation of everything (including water) for days, and/or the consumption of water but nothing else for weeks.

I feel incredibly uncomfortable with this idea, but I confess I haven't researched this area comprehensively. I'm mentioning it here because it is just another way for people to get confused about what they should be putting into their body. Luckily for you, that's where this book comes in to its own, because Jane and I have tried almost everything under the sun. So, any suggestions you are reading here are from real people who have no stake in leading you down the garden path.

One of the traps too many of us fell into in the quest to be skinny was the high-protein approaches such as the Atkin diet. Sure enough these diets are effective in terms of losing weight in the short term. The problem is that in the absence of carbohydrates and/or fats, our body is forced to use protein for energy. The main consequence of this is that we won't get nearly as much muscle building and tissue repair value from the protein we're consuming as we would if our intake of carbohydrates and fats was adequate. Meanwhile in the case of the high carbohydrate/low fat diets that were popular a while back, what you're losing as the number on your scales goes down, is muscle rather than fat.

The bottom line is that eating in a way that does not support your body to function well will leave you feeling lacklustre and drained. It will speed up the aging process, and predispose you to preventable diseases like diabetes, heart disease, blood pressure, arthritis, and the list goes on.

The main points I want you to take away from reading this chapter are to:

- Eat mindfully.
- Avoid processed foods as much as possible.
- Consume around 46 grams of protein every day.
- Consume at least 25 grams of fibre every day.
- Aim for carbohydrates to account for about half of your dietary intake with as much as possible being in the complex form.
- Minimize the intake of simple carbohydrates.
- Include as many antioxidant rich foods in your diet as possible, with at least 5 servings of vegetables and 2 servings of fruit per day.
- Limit fats to less than 25% of your total calories, with trans-fats being less than 10% of total fat consumption.
- Consistently exercise portion control.
- Use steaming or slow cooking rather than the high heat methods of grilling, frying, and barbequing because these will result in the production of AGEs.
- Drink at least two litres of water per day (or herbal teas if you prefer a warm liquid).
- Have a professional analyse the health of your gut if you are having any problems and take any recommended action to increase healthy gut flora.

WHAT IF I WANT TO LOSE WEIGHT?

Maintaining a healthy weight is important for your health from all perspectives. I'm often asked what a healthy weight actually means. I'm going to explain that to you with reference to the chart below. Among other things, the chart highlights the fact that we're not dealing with a one size fits all scenario here. So whatever you do, don't hold yourself up to the standard of an athlete if you're just the 'average' person who wants to set themselves up for a high level of general health.

www.bmi-calculator.net/body-fat-calculator/body-fat-chart.

Body Fat Percentage Categories

Classification	Women (% fat)	Men (% fat)
Essential Fat	10-12%	2-4%
Athletes	14-20%	6-13%
Fitness	21-24%	14-17%
Acceptable	25-31%	18-25%
Obese	32%+	25%

What I want to say here is that if the information in the chart forced you to realise you need to make some changes in your life, I have several ideas for you to take on board that I'll share with you in a moment. Don't be put off if you feel challenged by the idea of having to change. It's a well-known fact that humans don't usually like changing their behaviour, especially around food, but I promise you your body will thank you for it.

The first idea I want to flag is for you to set yourself up with a balanced approach to the amount of movement you do vis a vid the number and type of calories you put into your body. What's more, the diet you decide to follow needs to be linked to what your goals are. I can't possibly know the goals of everyone who's reading this book, but for the purpose of this exercise, I'm going to base what I say here on my experience of having 9 out of 10 clients who come to me for help wanting to lose weight.

You'll be learning a lot about exercise in Chapter 7, so all I'll say about exercise here is that what you want to be doing as a minimum is something that gets you up and moving every day, and something that will actively help in relation to fat loss, body tone and muscle gain two to three times per week.

So, here's what you need to know when it comes to making choices around what you eat from the point of view of losing weight.

Protein: Consume between 75 to 175 grams of protein per day.

Most people should eat between 1.0 to 1.5 grams of protein per kilo of their body weight. Eating enough protein helps prevent the breakdown of muscle so that the weight you lose is fat rather than muscle. Replacing 1 to 2 meals a day with a High Protein Shake will help to reduce your weight, while maintaining muscle tone. In a study where dieters doubled their protein intake, they reported experiencing a reduction in appetite, and they consumed fewer kilos than those in the control group.

Carbohydrates: Reduce your intake of simple carbohydrates and above all else avoid sugar and processed foods.

Burning fat can be achieved by reducing your intake of carbohydrates overall, and especially the simple carbohydrates that are found in processed foods. Ideally you want to be eating somewhere between 50 and 200g of carbohydrates depending on your kj breakeven point. The break-even point on average for women is about 8368 kj and for men about 11460 kj. Eat plenty of fibre-rich vegetables, but avoid grains, pasta, potatoes, rice, bread, junk food, high-glycaemic sugary carbs and all forms of sugar. Add berries or other fruits to your shake but do it sparingly as fruit has natural sugars in it. Totally avoid the high glycaemic index fruits like bananas and peaches.

Fats: Consume in the range of 40 to 90 grams of healthy fats per day.

You want to be favouring omega-3 fats over omega-6, although both are very important. An easy way for you to get a good balance of these is to cook with coconut oil, and use olive oil and/or flax seed oil on your salads. It's great to include avocado in your salads because the fat it provides is an excellent source of omega 3. To moderate your intake of omega-6 fats you need to consume things like safflower, sunflower and corn oil sparingly, if at all. Above all else, it's important to avoid the unhealthy fats that you'll be taking into your body if you eat fried food, as well as margarine and all hydrogenated oils that are known as trans fats.

AND WHAT ABOUT WATER:

Drinking an adequate amount of water every day is vital to your survival as a living being. That should be all I need to say really, but because I meet so many people who are dehydrated, I'm going to throw in a few good reasons to encourage you to drink plenty of water.

1. One of the incredibly helpful things that water does is boost metabolism in general, and our body's ability to burn fat in particular. A recent study found that drinking one glass of water increases the metabolic rate in healthy men and women by up to 30 percent. Conversely, even mild dehydration slows the metabolism down by as much as 3 percent. Studies also suggest that drinking one or two glasses of water before a meal will fill you up to an extent where you will naturally be inclined to eat less.
2. A six-year study published in the American Journal of Epidemiology found that people who drank around five glasses of water a day, were 41 percent less likely to die from a heart attack than those who drank less than two glasses.
3. Staying hydrated will make you less likely to get headaches, but if you do happen to get a headache, being well hydrated will decrease its intensity. Also drinking between eight to ten glasses of water per day has been shown to improve cognitive performance by as much as 30 percent. The other side of the coin is that a dehydration level of just 1 percent of your body weight is

thought to reduce mental performance, mostly in relation to short-term memory and focus.
4. Dehydration is the single most common cause of daytime fatigue. So, if your afternoon slump is more like a desperate need for an afternoon nap, having a glass of water is a much better alternative than a cup of coffee to boost your productivity through the tricky afternoon period.

My grandparents
William Sellick and Lillan Myrtle Price

In Capri, Amalfi Coast

Balance your Body,
Balance your Mind

At a Fund Raising event as
Coordinator of the
Chatswood Sheperd Centre

My beautiful children

My mother in the
Royal Auslralian Airforce

Didier and I on our #VanLife trip
around Australia

YogaNidra (The Waking Sleep)

Our wedding,
27th Jan 1990, Paris

My parent's wedding
5th July 1949, Sydney

My parents

Ballet days

My first book

My father, Stan Healy (top right)
with his parents and sibblings

Movement is medicine

1985 Women's
Australian Aerobic
Championship

2017 Women Economic Forum,
New Deli, India

Teaching YogaPilates
Fusion in schools

CHAPTER SIX

BRAIN AND GUT HEALTH

As you read previously, oxidation and inflammation are the two main culprits when it comes to illness and premature aging. So it will come as no surprise to you to hear them come up again in the context of brain and gut health. I've been researching this topic for a while now, and I'm surprised the link between gut health, depression and dementia is not getting the kind of attention it deserves.

From where I sit, it makes a lot of sense to do whatever we need to do to enable our heart and blood vessels to work properly. They need to be working properly to deliver blood and nutrients efficiently to our brain. That's why a morning shot of caffeine is not only beneficial as an energy booster because it also protects the brain. I promise I'm not sharing this information with you because I want to justify my regular almond milk coffee that I have first thing every morning. I'm sharing it with you because I want to highlight the fact that our susceptibility to neurodegenerative diseases like Alzheimer's has been shown to decline if we drink coffee. This is because caffeine reduces inflammation, which in turn allows the free flow of blood through the body.

Because the cells in the brain are fat-based, any changes to lipid (fat) metabolism will affect the health of the brain. So it's a good idea to have your blood lipids (HDL, LDL and triglycerides) and your cholesterol levels tested yearly. You also want to be keeping your blood pressure within the healthy range of 120/80 or less. Addressing issues with your weight is important too because adipose tissue (otherwise known as body fat) is a metabolically active tissue that secretes hormones and cell signalling molecules that are no good for the brain. Too much fat (particularly visceral fat around our internal organs) leads to higher levels of inflammation and metabolic disruption. That's why it's worth eating foods that are found in the Mediterranean, Japanese and Scandinavian diets because they are rich in antioxidants, B vitamins and anti-inflammatory fats, which are beneficial from the point of view of maintaining a healthy brain as well as a healthy body.

Phytonutrients are the natural compounds in plants that protect them from viruses and bacteria. These highly nutritious substances explain why a plant-based diet is great for our overall health, and in particular, our brain health. As a general rule, what you should be doing is maximising your intake of colourful fruits and vegetables, including plenty of the dark green leafy ones. These are beneficial because they are full of vitamins, minerals, phytonutrients and antioxidants. Many world cuisines and traditional diets also include herbs and spices like curcumin (turmeric), saffron, cinnamon, garlic and ginger. These all have protective properties that help the body to avoid going into an inflammatory state. There are plenty of supplements you can buy that provide these substances as well, however supplementing these compounds doesn't seem to deliver the same health benefits as actually eating the fruit and vegetables they're contained within.

I cringe when I think about the low-fat diets that many of us bought into in the late 80s and early 90s. It breaks my heart to think about how much I missed out on by excluding things that I love like almonds, peanuts, and avocado. This was a sacrifice I was prepared to make because I believed that they were the kinds of foods that would make me fat back in the day. Fortunately, we now know that the monounsaturated fat in foods like these are not only good for us, but that they are absolutely critical to maintaining the health of our brain.

Meanwhile diets that contain high levels of saturated-fats seem to make it harder for us to clear beta-amyloid from the brain, as well as being detrimental to our circulation. So these are the foods we need to be minimising or eliminating from our diet completely. Sadly, the average person typically consumes way too many saturated fats in processed foods that deliver a double whammy. They are not only devoid of the kinds of nutritional properties fresh foods have, but they are also high in damaging substances like salt, sugar, trans fats, and preservatives. This is a terrible combination because it increases inflammation which is the perfect environment for neurodegeneration to occur.

Another thing to be mindful of when you're making decisions about whether to cut processed foods out of your life in favour of cooking your own food in a healthful way, is that when cooking oils are heated to very high temperatures (in the case of deep frying for example) they form the compounds I mentioned earlier called AGEs. AGEs are most often found in highly processed foods, meats, full fat cheeses, and foods cooked by grilling, frying, and roasting. AGEs have a long half-life in the body, and seem to promote oxidative stress and inflammation, as well as contributing to the development of beta-amyloid plaque that we see in the brains of dementia sufferers.

The other thing to do to keep your brain healthy is to make sure you are getting enough of the B group vitamins through your diet, or via supplementation if it's not possible for you to get it through the food you eat. B6, folic acid, and B12 are particularly important for brain health. We get the B vitamins from a wide variety of foods such as whole grains, beans, legumes, fruits, vegetables, meats and fish.

The bottom line is that you're probably fine if you are eating a varied diet that includes a broad range of animal and plant foods, and you're not actively depleting your B vitamins by drinking too much alcohol. If you have an exclusively plant-based diet it's worth considering supplementation, particularly in relation to vitamin B12.

The centrality of the gut to our overall health and our brain health in particular has never been better understood than it is now. Researchers estimate that about one-quarter of the people who have celiac disease also have neurological or mental health issues as well. These often take the form of depression and anxiety. The connection here is that damage to the intestinal lining allows pathogens to enter our circulation. This causes a cascade effect with the body's immune system being activated, which in turn leads to inflammation that destroys healthy tissue, including the tissue in the brain.

The microbiome is our body's inner ecosystem. When all is well, our gut is full of good bacteria along with helpful viruses and fungi. When all is not well, pathogenic bacteria will be present. That's a problem because this kind of bacteria secretes compounds such as amyloids and endotoxins which increase inflammation and contribute to the formation of plaques and tangles in the brain. The bottom line is that if our gut microbiome is out of balance, whether it's the result of the overuse of antibiotics, or something else that harms the delicate balance within the system, it is likely that neurological and other health problems will result.

Vitamin D is best known for its contribution to bone health, but recent research suggests that it could also provide a range of healthful affects in relation to our brain as well. Vitamin D is thought to contribute to neuroplasticity, calcium balance, and metabolism. Getting enough sunlight every day and consuming foods that are high in vitamin D such as eggs, seafood, liver, and certain mushrooms, is the best way to make sure that you don't become vitamin D deficient.

Controversy around the question of alcohol and brain health is alive and well. Without wading too far into contested terrain here, I feel comfortable in saying that having the occasional alcoholic drink, especially if it's red wine, shouldn't be too problematic as long as your approach to diet and exercise is sound.

Another thing to take into account is the matter of how much stress you're exposed to daily. While our brains like, and even need a little bit of stress, chronic stress is detrimental to the health of our brain. Over time, prolonged distress and anxiety can interfere with learning, memory, decision-making and other important cognitive functions. This is why I love introducing my clients to Yoga Nidra which is the wonderful tool to de-stress that I shared with you earlier.

It's also important that you don't take the amount of metal you are exposed to for granted. For example, copper has been found in amyloid plaques, and the accumulation of amyloid plaques between the nerve cells in the brain is a precursor to Alzheimer's disease. Furthermore, things like mercury, lead, cadmium, aluminium, polychlorinated biphenyls, pesticides, and arsenic will accumulate in the body and contribute to neurological problems that may not be noticeable for a very long time. It's not known exactly what role these toxic substances play, but given their known neurotoxic effects, there's no doubt it's worth doing whatever you can to avoid them as much as possible. If you've never given it a second thought before, you're likely to be surprised and possibly alarmed when you realise how many harmful chemicals are in your house in the way of cleaning products, pesticides, paint fumes and heavy metals of all kinds.

On the upside, current research is suggesting that consuming alpha-lipoic acid which is found in things like yeast, liver, kidney, spinach, broccoli, and potatoes will increase the effectiveness of a class of drugs called cholinesterase. These drugs are used to slow down the mental decline experienced by people with Alzheimer's.

Research also suggests that carnitine which is found in nearly every cell in our body might play a protective role against cognitive decline. Other substances like choline and uridine are necessary for the formation of synapses, so eating good quality organic eggs is beneficial to the health of our brain too. Selenium which is a powerful antioxidant is another substance that's worth being aware of. Selenium which is found in things like Brazil nuts, whole grains and leafy green vegetables is beneficial in small frequent doses. Zinc is also excellent for brain health, however on a cautionary note, it's important to avoid consuming more zinc than your body needs because it will interfere with your ability to metabolise copper.

Ginkgo Biloba has long been touted as a supplement that improves cognitive functioning. While it appears to be safe, and has been shown to improve attention and mood, there is not a lot of evidence to suggest there are any benefits for the health of the brain per se connected with using Ginkgo Biloba.

A point I really want to drive home here is that just like all the other muscles in the body, our brain works better the more we use it. Using it includes all sorts of activities in addition to the more obvious ones like learning a foreign language, doing crossword puzzles, or taking a course in a challenging field that you know nothing about. Things like travelling and meeting new people are incredibly beneficial as well. In fact, staying socially connected and engaged, and finding a sense of purpose, are all important when it comes to avoiding the ravages that aging can bring to bear on the health of our brain and our wellbeing overall.

So let me ask you:

- Do you feel 'connected' to others and to your life's purpose?
- Are you engaged and interested in the world around you?
- Do you have a range of close, supportive, and meaningful relationships in your life?
- Do you feel like you are able to make a difference and/or a contribution?

If you answered no to any of the questions above, I want you to think about one thing you could do today to turn things around. You'll find a lot more to think about when you get to the chapter on relationships coming up soon. In a sense, answering the questions here will be warming you up for what's to come.

At the end of the day, physical health includes brain health. Therefore, anything you do to improve your physical health will contribute to the health of your brain as well. The kinds of things I have in mind here are:

- Not smoking
- Maintaining a healthy weight

- Getting adequate amounts of good quality sleep
- Drinking alcohol in moderation, if at all
- Consuming adequate amounts of colourful fruits and vegetables
- Consuming enough lean protein
- Including enough healthy fats in your diet
- Eating as wide a variety of foods as possible
- Getting regular exercise
- Managing your stress
- Minimising your exposure to chemicals
- Taking supplements if required
- Exercising and moving your body to the extent that it will increase the amount of oxygen in the blood that is constantly flowing into your brain.

I'm going to leave the last word here to Anna Guz who is an expert on gut health. Anna and I paired up to run a series of workshops prior to Covid. According to Anna, "Your Gut Health has a direct positive impact on:

- Your mood and happiness
- Anxiety, depression, irritability, frustration, anger
- Fighting infection and inflammation
- Energy and motivation
- Maintaining hormonal and brain health
- Controlling appetite and cravings
- Losing weight, keeping it off, and more.

CHAPTER SEVEN

THE EXERCISE WE DO

This chapter is not just about exercise. It's about a range of things that will support you in your quest to establish healthy habits around movement. These things include goal setting, breathing, and mindset. Basically, this chapter is all about setting up an environment that will make it possible for you to break through any barriers that might pop up as you work on changing your more or less sedentary lifestyle into an active one. Even if you don't fall directly into the sedentary group, you will still benefit from the information I'm sharing with you here.

I'm writing this as a person who's been involved in the fitness industry for over 40 years. The industry was in its infancy when I first started out. I guess that's not technically true because the history of physical fitness and exercise goes back a very long way. But when I got into the industry in the 1980s there were no television shows like "The Biggest Loser" taking people from one extreme to the other by dropping massive amounts of weight in a ridiculously short period of time. And there were no social media channels charting the progress of 80+ year old women with abs to die for, or Instagram influencers with tiny waists and sculptured butts. Nor were there the kind of entrepreneurial people we see today who preside over fitness empires that afford them lifestyles of the rich and famous.

While I've more than kept pace with the landscape that's changed dramatically over the last four decades, the foundations of the programs I offer have remained more or less the same. My focus is, and will always be, based on getting sustainable results for the people who tap into my unique programs. These programs are about skilling my clients up to create the very best conditions for their body and mind to thrive in.

Sadly, there is no shortage of people who are struggling with their health. One of the main groups I work with are concerned about the shape their body is in. For the most part, the shape their body is in is attributable to the fact that they are either 1) eating the wrong foods, and/or 2) not taking account of the fact that what they put into their body as energy via the food they eat has to be equal to or less than the amount of energy they burn during the course of the day.

So it stands to reason that incorporating exercise in our life makes a whole lot of sense. I'm sorry to have to be the one to tell you this, but there is no miracle cure that will make it possible for you to take all of the extra weight you're carrying around off without any effort on your part. The same is true when it comes to increasing your flexibility and muscle mass.

In fact, the solution to any problems you might be having with your body starts with aligning your mindset with the goal of achieving a healthful solution. It's not uncommon for me to rant and rave a bit when I talk about the confusion and expense I see people going through with the plethora of weight-loss diets and scams that push them into spending hundreds and thousands of dollars on programs that simply don't work. They don't work because the strategy health seekers need is one that is aligned with who they are and suits their particular circumstances.

It's really important to have goals in place when you're looking to change the results you are getting. Goals help because change is not something humans are naturally comfortable with. Setting a goal that is achievable, and has some level of accountability embedded in it, will make it much easier for you to stay focussed, and avoid being derailed by things like perfectionism, procrastination, or social comparison.

If you have a lot of weight to lose, then it might take you a year or more to reach your goal. Rather than feeling dispirited about that, I want you to find a way to appreciate the fact that your body and your mind need time to make a complete and sustainable change to ensure you don't get sucked into a toxic dieting pattern where your weight goes up and down like a yoyo. This is a dangerous way to live, and a trap that way too many people fall into I'm afraid.

As I say this to you now, I know only too well that I'm part of an industry that can be very skewed when it comes to giving advice about goals and standards. Unfortunately, it's not uncommon for people to turn up to gyms and coaching programs and be given completely unrealistic and sometimes even dangerous advice. In fact, it makes me sad to reflect on the fallout from the commercialisation of the fitness landscape that often works against the very people who need it the most. For my part, I am incredibly proud of the work I do with my practical pro-aging approach to wellbeing. And my heart is full to overflowing when I think about some of the wonderful testimonials I've received over the years.

You'll see a range of case studies where people talk about the fabulous results they've achieved in the Appendix section. I don't share these results with you to boast. I share them so that you will be inspired by the results that people just like you have been able to achieve with commitment, sensible guidance and solid support.

I feel blessed to be able to help my clients to heal on both an emotional and physical level through exercise. I especially love it when the light goes on for those who may have been inactive for decades. When these people finally discover the beautiful energy and satisfaction that comes from having an active body and mind, their life is changed forever. Some of them don't get to that place without a fight, but on some level they know they simply can't afford to walk away from the need to do something about getting their body moving so they can be healthier and happier, and go on to live in a much more healthful state for longer than they otherwise would. They have a right to feel gratified because they are head and shoulders above the others who buy into the inevitability of a stereotypical old age where their body is riddled with disease, and their quality of life is terrible.

I don't care what age you are now, or what state your body is in. If you take nothing else away from reading this book, I want you to leave with a determination to do whatever it takes to claim your right to a fabulous future. I wish I could remember who said this, because I would love to attribute these wonderful words to them. The words are - "Make sure your past isn't shouting so loudly that you can't hear your future inviting you in."

You might be surprised to find the first thing we're going to be focussing on is something you do every moment of every day. That thing is breathing.

BREATHING:

I suspect this is not the first thing that sprang to mind when you thought about what might be included in a chapter on exercise. I've included it here because the ability to focus on and control your breath has a lot more to do with the results you get from exercising than you might imagine. In fact, the breathing techniques I'm about to share with you have far reaching implications for your overall health. So I'm going to invite you to look at your breath as a foundational aspect of your body's ability to get fitter and better.

Taking just a few minutes a day to focus on your breath will not only calm your body and your mind. It will also revitalise your spirit. If you're like many of the people I meet who say they don't have time to dedicate to their health, then I'm afraid you're going to have to change your tune, because at the most basic level all you need to do is focus your attention on taking three deep breaths while you're driving to and from work, or perhaps while you're doing the shopping, or in your lunch break, or when you're visiting the bathroom, or whatever.

Believe me, even just three deep long inhales and exhales while you're at the traffic lights will take the edge off the stress that is sitting in your body. I really want you to give this a go, because I know it will only take a minute or so for you to get a taste of how much better you'll feel when you have a decent flow of oxygen in your body.

Beyond the very basic intervention I just mentioned, I'd love you to experiment with one or more of the wonderful breathing techniques I'm sharing with you on the following pages. If this works well for you, you might even like to consider bringing family members on board to try it out as well.

Equal Breathing, or Sama Vritti Pranayama

The first breathing technique for you to experiment with is well known for having a calming and re-energising effect on the body. It also has the ability to help us focus our mind. This technique is called Equal Breathing, or Sama Vritti Pranayama.

The steps involved in this breathing technique are:

1. Sit in a comfortable, cross-legged position on the floor, or in a chair, or with your back up against the wall.
2. Close your eyes and begin noticing your natural breath, without trying to change anything.
3. Then begin a slow count to four as you inhale. And slowly count to four as you exhale. NB: The point of this exercise is to match the length of your inhale and exhale. By all means you can experiment with changing the number that you count to, but make sure the length of your inhale and the length of your exhale remain the same.
4. Continue breathing this way for several minutes.

Alternate Nostril Breathing, or Nadi Sodhana

Another technique for you to try is one of the most popular breathing techniques I teach in the programs I run for schools. This one is called Alternate Nostril Breathing, or Nadi Sodhana. It is known for its effect on our ability to balance, relax, and calm down.

The steps involved in Alternate Nostril Breathing are:

1. Sit in a comfortable cross-legged position.
2. Using your right hand, fold your index and middle fingers into your palm, leaving your thumb, ring finger, and little finger sticking up.
3. Bring your thumb to the right side of your nose. and your ring finger to the left side.
4. Close off your right nostril with your thumb, and inhale through your left nostril.
5. Close off your left nostril with your ring finger, as you open and exhale through your right nostril.
6. Inhale through your right nostril, then close off your right nostril with your thumb.
7. Open and exhale through your left nostril.
8. Inhale through your left nostril.
9. Continue alternating in this way for 5 to 10 times.

Cooling Breath, or Shitali Pranayama

The Cooling Breath is also known as The Tongue Roll. This technique cools the body, so it's great in hot weather, especially if you're doing intense exercise.

The steps involved in the Cooling Breath are:

1. Sit in a comfortable cross-legged position on the floor if possible, or on a chair if necessary.
2. Take two or three deep inhales and exhales through your nose to prepare.
3. Roll your tongue, curling the sides in towards the center to form a tube. Then stick the end of your tongue out between your pursed lips. If you can't roll your tongue, just hold your lips making a small "o" shape with your mouth.
4. Inhale through the tube of the tongue.
5. Exhale through the nose.
6. Repeat this process 5 to 10 times.

Ocean Breath, or Ujjayi Pranayama

Ocean Breath is also known as the Hissing Breath and the Victorious Breath. This technique concentrates and directs the breath, giving your Yoga and Pilates practice in particular extra power and focus.

The steps involved in Ocean Breath are:

1. Inhale and exhale deeply through your mouth.
2. On the exhales, start to tone the back of your throat, by slightly constricting the passage of air. It might help to imagine you are fogging up a pair of glasses.
3. Once you're comfortable with the exhale, start to apply the same toning of your throat on the inhales. This is where the name of the breath comes from because it actually sounds like the ocean.
4. When you are able to control your throat on both the inhale and the exhale, close your mouth and start breathing through your nose. Continue applying the same toning to your throat that you applied when your mouth was open. The breath will still make a loud noise coming in and out of the nose. This is Ujjayi breath.

HOW TO START TO GET YOUR BODY MOVING:

Now that you have some breathing exercises to keep your body oxygenated, we're going to look at the question of what you need to do to get your body moving and build your fitness. There are three key goals that your fitness program needs to address. I will explain each of these to you in turn below. The goals are:

1. To build your cardio fitness.
2. To build your strength.
3. To build your flexibility.

Cardio:

What happens when we build our cardio fitness is that our body becomes more efficient at absorbing oxygen. So when you put your body under the increased demand of a cardio workout, you're priming it to be able to take in more oxygen with less effort, thus improving your chances of avoiding cardiovascular disease. Cardio training is also beneficial from the point of view of cholesterol. It improves the amount of HDL relative to the dangerous LDL levels in the bloodstream. In fact, research reveals that a simple shift from a low level of cardio fitness to a moderate level can reduce the risk of death due to cardiovascular disease by as much as 50%.

The basics of an effective cardio regime include a warm-up and cool-down phase at either end of the workout phase. What you want to be doing during the workout phase is maintaining the level of intensity you're working at to between 55% and 90% of your maximum heart rate. You can calculate your basic maximum heart rate by subtracting your age from 220. It would be ideal to start with at least three 20-minute sessions of cardio a week and work your way up to three 60-minute sessions from there. If 20-minutes seems daunting at first, you can break it down to two 10-minute sessions a day while you build your fitness and your confidence up. Basically, you should aim for whatever is going to get you off the starting blocks and build up from there.

Examples of cardio exercise you might like to think about taking up include jogging, power walking, cycling, aerobics, and aqua aerobics. The bottom line is that f you aim to regularly do whatever you get some enjoyment from doing, you will increase your chances of establishing a sustainable fitness program that will see you keeping your body fit and active throughout your life. At present HIIT (High Intensity Interval Training) is very popular. Research shows that it is excellent for the over 55's from the point of view of maintaining muscle strength and increasing heart health. The fact that it is done in short quick bursts of around 30 seconds per exercise followed by a break of 30 seconds, means that HIIT jump starts your body and keeps the oxygen and blood circulating really well.

I should add the caveat that it's possible that none of these options tick the box of being enjoyable for you in the beginning. But if you approach this project with curiosity and persevere for a little while, my guess is that eventually you'll stumble on something that feels inherently right for you, or at least more right than the other options do.

STRENGTH AND ENDURANCE:

Muscular endurance training improves the supply of oxygen to the muscles so that you're able to train for longer before lactic acid builds up. Meanwhile muscular strength training increases the cross section of muscle because of the small tears to the tissues that take place at the cellular level when you train. To maximise these kinds of benefits you need to 1) eat enough protein, and 2) rest between sessions to let the muscle tears repair themselves. It's the tearing and repairing that improves the strength of the muscles you are training.

A basic resistance training schedule that combines both strength and endurance includes one set of 8 to 12 repetitions of 8 to 10 different exercises that work all the major muscle groups. You could start by using lighter weights with a higher number of repetitions and build the weight up gradually from there. What you want to be aiming for is to be working at an intensity that brings you to the edge of your ability. In other words, don't make it too easy for yourself, but don't go overboard by making it too hard either.

With resistance training you might be using your body weight, exercise machines, or free weights for resistance. Once you get started you'll be entitled to feel great in the knowledge that you're doing something to build muscle and maintain bone density and strength as you move through your life. This matters because it's well known that these things start to decline as we age if we don't make a commitment to do what it takes to stop that from happening. Endurance and strength training also provide benefits from the point of view of increasing our metabolic rate, decreasing our blood pressure, and tipping the balance in favour of healthy cholesterol.

There's no need to worry about bulking up and looking too masculine when you put energy into strength training. I mention this because some of the women who approach me wanting to get fitter express that concern. Bulking up is not a problem for women because we simply don't have enough testosterone to build muscle in the way men do. For us, strength training is going to improve our muscle mass and decrease our chances of getting osteoporosis. So rather than becoming muscle bound, what we're able to achieve is a lean, well-toned appearance like Jane Fonda and Helen Mirren have. Women like these beautifully counteract the stereotypical idea of aging that most of us were brought up to believe was our fate.

FLEXIBILITY:

This aspect of fitness is really important as we age. I say that because it is key to being able to maintain independence through mobility and strength. Modalities like Yoga and Pilates work by strategically stretching muscles beyond their original length at the same time as engaging our breath to relax our body, whilst strengthening it as well. You'll find a number of exercises focussed on building your flexibility toward the end of this chapter.

As I mentioned earlier, one of the most important things to consider when you're thinking about starting an exercise program is to find something you enjoy doing. It's worth thinking about finding a group of people who are likely to become a close-knit tribe to keep you motivated, focussed, accountable, and above all else, enjoying the journey. I see no point in starting off on the back foot, so if yoga is not your thing, and Pilates feels too hard for you to start with, and a repetitive group class strikes you as boring, then find the 'thing' that feels most comfortable and/or inspiring to you. It could be anything from salsa classes to a full-on military-style bootcamp approach. No matter what it is that you decide to do, as long as you actually do it, you will start to feel much stronger, fitter, and better in a relatively short period of time.

Joseph Pilates who is the father of Pilates said something that really rings true for me. He said that "If your spine is inflexible and stiff at 30, you are old. And if it is flexible at 60, you are young". Another way he puts it is that "we are only as young as our spines are flexible." A big problem that worries me is the legacy of sitting for long periods at a time, often crouched over a computer. A by-product of this is premature ageing that manifests in a lack of flexibility in the spine. I've developed a specific set of exercises for anyone who finds themselves stuck in an office environment. You will find this at bodyandbalance.com.

For now, I just want to reiterate that an exercise program that includes more movement and less sitting will put you in a much better position from the point of view of your health in general, and your longevity in particular.

One of the less obvious benefits of getting your body moving is that regular exercise has been shown to decrease feelings of depression, anxiety and stress. This has to do with the endorphins and other hormones like serotonin and norepinephrine that are released when we exercise. It also has to do with the fact that we just feel better when our body is strong and flexible. And as you learnt in the last chapter, exercise is also essential for brain health because it promotes the flow of oxygen and blood to that wonderful organ called our brain that we rely on for just about everything.

Recent research has shown that no matter what intensity the exercise or physical activity you do is, positive mood changes will occur. For example, one study in the US asked 40 healthy men and women who normally exercised a minimum of 30 minutes 3 times per week, to either continue exercising, or to stop exercising altogether for two weeks. Those who stopped exercising reported experiencing an increase in depression, anxiety, dark moods, and/or feeling stressed.

There are just so many great reasons to exercise including the fact that:

- It contributes to the maintenance of a healthy weight by boosting metabolism.
- It assists in maintaining muscle mass.
- It improves our mood and reduces the risk of mental health issues such as depression and anxiety.
- It improves cognitive functioning and the health of our brain.
- It makes us more creative and productive.

- It helps us to feel more empowered and confident.
- It is great for bone strength and helps to prevent osteoporosis.
- It increases energy levels and improves sleep.
- It reduces the risk of chronic diseases such as cancer and diabetes.
- It is pro-ageing (or anti-ageing, depending on which way you look at being healthy for longer).
- In certain circumstances it also provides a sense of community and belonging.

  It's worth noting that the benefits of exercise increase if you schedule in more frequent activity, rather than intense bouts of less-frequent activity. This is great because it:
- Reverses the rate of cell deterioration that takes place as we age.
- Decreases the loss of synapses in the brain.
- Increases the protective neurotrophic (neuron growth) factors.
- Improves the insulin signalling pathways.
- Decreases inflammation.
- Increases the levels of brain-derived neurotrophic factor (BDNF), which is important for learning and memory.

Below you will see three ideas I want to throw into the mix to support you to make this the time that you finally turn your life around by getting your body moving. I worded the last sentence the way I did because I often see people who are at the end of their tether. They tell me they've tried everything, and nothing seems to stick. I totally understand how dispiriting it can be to keep stopping and starting without getting any appreciable results, so I've set the programs I have available up in a way that has made them particularly sticky. But for those of you who don't feel like the time is right to sign up for a program per se, I want to urge you to do these three things.

1. Join a community

You are now an honorary member of my *Body and Balance* online community by virtue of having bought this book. I set this community up because the more connected we feel, the more likely we are to stick to our exercise program, even if our motivation starts to wane. We love welcoming new people into our group, and would love to know more about you, so why not log on to our Facebook group and introduce yourself here www.facebook.com/groups/1673370326249752/.

2. Establish a routine

If there's one thing I've learnt over the decades I've been working in the fitness industry, it's that an on-again off-again approach doesn't usually work. The best way to maintain optimum wellbeing and reduce the risk of preventable health problems like obesity, diabetes, muscle wastage and more, is to aim for a minimum of 30 minutes of moderate-intensity physical activity on most (and preferably all) days of the week. As far as joining an exercise class of one kind or other goes, my advice is to just jump in and give it a go. Whether you are committing to one, three or more sessions per week, really commit to the session time you pick, because before too long it will become second nature to turn up without having to fight the battle of procrastination every time. In fact, you'll probably even feel a little bit lost if you ever wind up having to miss a session.

3. Establish a positive mindset

The bottom line is that if you tell yourself you hate exercise, then you will hate exercise. If you're using exercise as a way to punish yourself for eating too much, then you will hate exercise. If you are only exercising because you want to achieve an unrealistic weight-loss goal, then you will hate exercise. But if you are exercising because you know it's part of your plan to nurture and care for yourself, then you will learn to love exercise. And believe me, you will love watching your body evolve into a strong, toned, well-functioning home for your wonderful heart and soul to feel great in.

BUT WILL IT WORK FOR ME:

I have women coming to me who are aged anywhere between 30 and 90, who sheepishly admit they've been a couch potato for years or even decades. They don't always use the words couch potato. They might use words like slack, or lazy, or busy, or some other word that sums up the fact that they desperately need help to get their body moving again.

A common thread through all these women's stories is a simmering sense of fear about the impact their lack of movement is having on their body, coupled with a sense of doom about their body breaking down if they don't do something about it soon. I'm happy to say that if these women get up the courage to sign up and start working with me, then it only takes a couple of weeks before they start to feel a difference. Then in a couple of months they start to notice real changes in the way their body is looking and how much energy they have.

These are the kinds of results that come out of strategically moving our body regularly. On the following pages you will find a set of basic exercises that will give you a very good place to start if you've been a bit of a couch potato for most of your life. You'll notice that I've included a section called 'watch points' with each of the exercises. I've done this because technique is important, both from the point of view of avoiding injury, and from the point of view of getting the best bang for your buck in terms of the results you achieve. If you're in any doubt after looking at any of the descriptions you read, come on over to my website at bodyandbalance.com.au. That's where you'll find videos showing you exactly how to do all of these exercises safely and effectively.

It's also very important to take note of the contraindications that I've included with each of the exercises. In some cases, it's unwise to do certain exercises in particular ways. For example, if you have back problems of any kind, it's unlikely that a 'standard' Spine Twist without any modification would be a good idea for you.

The first 10 exercises I'll be talking you through are part of my Yoga-Pilates Fusion® Program. One of the things these exercises do is heat up your core body temperature to prepare you for the strengthening, lengthening, co-ordination, breathing, and core stability movements that follow.

We start with a strategic warm up phase.

THE WARM UP PHASE

Focussing on your breath is very important in these exercises. It will help you to maintain balance in your body and mind, as well as maintaining heat in your body. As we warm up, we release sweat through our sweat glands. This helps to detoxify and cleanse our blood and tissues, and improve our circulation while balancing our mind.

Body Alignment, Posture and Breath Check

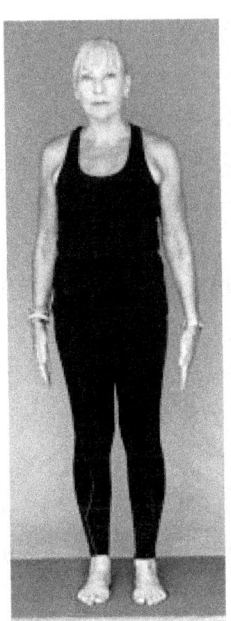
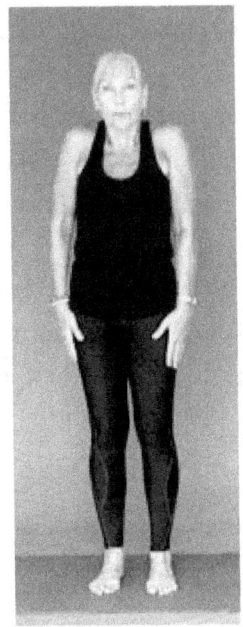
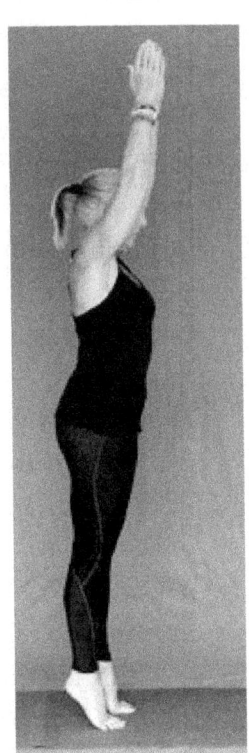

Aim:

The aim here is to bring your focus and awareness to your breath and your posture. The core foundational pose in YogaPilates Fusion is the Mountain Pose. We start with this pose to gain awareness of the alignment of our posture, core, balance and breathing.

Technique:

- Stand with your feet parallel and hip distance apart, and your body tall, strong and upright, while your toes are spread and your arms are by your side, close your eyes and focus inward.

- Breathing in through your nose and out through your mouth. Lift your toes up pushing your heels into the mat, standing taller.
- Then drop your toes gently balancing evenly on both feet.
- Visualise moving the energy up through your ankles and shins.
- When you come to your knees, soften them, lift your kneecaps, and visualise drawing your thighs to your centre to engage your core.
- Gently lift your pelvic floor muscles at the base of your core.
- Imagine a corset or wide belt with 10 holes around your lumbar spine meeting at the front of your body between your navel and pubic bone.
- Inhale, and as you exhale tighten the imaginary belt to the 10th hole or 100% to flatten out your tummy by scooping it in (not sucking it in). Inhale and on the exhale loosen the imaginary belt to the 3rd hole. This will bring you to minimal core engagement of 30%.
- Breathe in to fill your lungs. Imagine filling each space between your ribs and around your ribcage as you expand your lung capacity. Then breathe out keeping your ribcage broadened.
- Lift and drop your shoulders forming a V shape in your back, lengthen your neck and the crown of your head toward the ceiling.
- Inhale, rise up onto your toes with your eyes closed and your arms reaching toward the ceiling as you focus on your breath and balance. Repeat this three times.

Watch Points:

- Keep your feet parallel and be conscious of the alignment of your body.

Contraindications:

- Dizziness,
- Ankle and shoulder issues.

Spine Twist (standing)

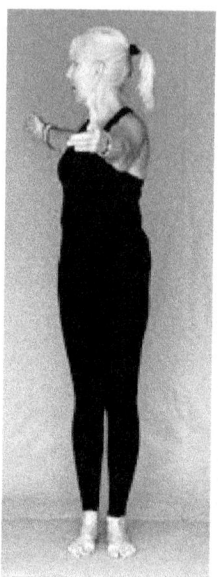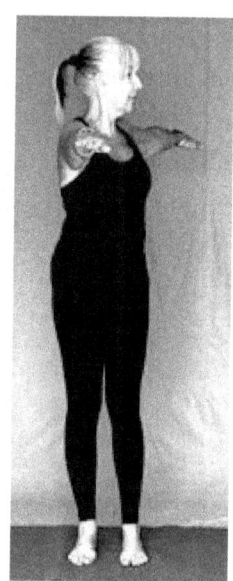

Aim:

The aim of this exercise is to rotate and lengthen your spine. Twisting your spine is wonderful for detoxification because it gently massages your internal organs. Inhaling helps to lengthen your spine, while exhaling helps with the rotation.

Technique:

- Inhale and stretch your arms out to shoulder height while turning your upper body to the right, looking back at your right arm on the exhale.

- Exhale and lift up onto your toes for balance, then lower your feet and lower your arms to look back at the left arm with your spine twisted.
- Repeat this process twice on each side.

Watch Points:

- Make sure you do not twist your lower limbs, and keep your knees, ankles and feet in parallel alignment.

Contraindications:

- Spinal issues such as herniated disc, pinched nerves, rib injuries, shoulder injuries.

Lateral Stretch

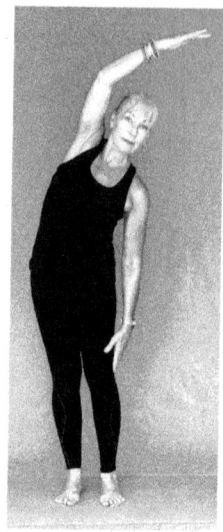

Aim:

This exercise continues the spinal mobilisation that we started with the Spine Twist. However, this time we are working on the lateral plane.

Technique:

- As you breathe in, lengthen your spine and take your left arm over your head. Then reach your right arm down the side of your body as you breath out.
- Repeat this on the other side.
- Repeat the whole process four times.
- To make this more challenging you might like to hold the lift longer and bring your bottom arm up to meet your top arm.

Watch Points:

- Make sure you maintain the correct posture with the arm that is over your head (not drifting toward the front of your face).

Contraindications:

- Spinal injuries, osteoporosis, shoulder injuries.

THE EXERCISE PHASE

Following on from the warmup phase, these exercises are a combination of traditional yoga poses that create body heat and prepare the muscles for the more intense Pilates based exercises. These will increase your heart rate, core muscle temperature, and circulation, and enable you to make the mind/body connection.

The first few poses in this set of exercises are based on Hatha Yoga. These are the body heating poses. While maintaining the breath and flow, you will be releasing tightness, stiffness and tension in your muscles. None of these poses are held for long, and if you experience any discomfort, I want you to listen to your body and move out of the pose using your breath, while adjusting the intensity of the stretch and/or twist.

NB: What we are moving into with the Warrior 2 Pose now, is a set of five specific exercises. After the Warrior 2 Pose, you will move on to the Side Angle Pose, Reverse Warrior Pose, Triangle Pose, and Reverse Triangle Pose. Then you will loop back and complete these five exercises again focusing on the other side of your body.

Warrior 2 Pose

Aim:

The aim of this pose is to stretch and open your hips, joints and thigh muscles. It's also wonderful from the point of view of strengthening the muscles in your shoulders, arms, spine, back, legs, and feet, as well as your gluteal and abdominal muscles. The underlying intention of this pose is to increase strength and positive energy.

Technique:

- Breathing in and out through your nose, keep your feet parallel and step them out to a wide stance (about 90cms apart).
- Take your arms out wide to shoulder height.
- Drop your shoulders down and lengthen your arms.
- Turn your right foot out and line your heel up with the middle of your left foot.
- Keep your torso facing the front while your left knee is bent, and make sure you keep your knee over your shin and your toes visible beyond the knee bend.

- Use your inner thigh muscles to stretch your heels away from each other.
- Turn your head to face the right arm and gaze along the middle finger of your right hand while lengthening the left arm.

Watch Points:

- Maintain alignment with your arms lengthened, shoulders dropped, and shoulder blades drawn down, while your neck is lengthened, and your feet are parallel.
- You can modify this by coming out of the knee bend while maintaining the arm stretch.

Contraindications:

- Knee, hip, neck and shoulder issues or injuries.

Side Angle Pose

Aim:

The aim of this pose is to open your chest, stretch your ribcage and increase flexibility and strength in your ankles, knees, thighs and hips.

Technique:

- Breathing in and out gently, imagine drawing your navel toward your spine, lengthening your spine and lower back.
- Breathe in, take your right arm to your right thigh and lift up out of your shoulder while reaching over and lengthening your left arm along your left ear and over your head.
- Keep your neck long and gently turn your gaze toward your left armpit.
- Lift and feel the expansion of your chest in this lateral position.
- Inhale and float your torso up to prepare for the Reverse Warrior pose.

Watch Points:

- Keep an eye on your alignment especially the angle of your knee, your head, and the tip of your hand which must be in line with the middle of your foot.

Contraindications:

- Knee, neck and shoulder issues.

Reverse Warrior

Aim:

The aim of this pose is to continue the flow with your breath, while working your oblique abdominal muscles, spine and legs.

Technique:

- Inhale and exhale through your nose.
- Keeping your legs in the same position as they were for the Side Angle Pose, breathe in and float your left arm down towards the centre of your left straight leg while you open your chest and lift your right arm.
- Look towards your right armpit while inhaling and exhaling through your nose.

- Release and turn to face the front bringing your feet back to parallel.

Watch Points:

- Make sure your knee is positioned over your ankle, and your turned foot is in alignment with your parallel foot.
- If your legs are getting tired you can bring your feet back to hip distance apart with a step or a jump (depending on your strength and fitness level).

Contraindications:

- Neck, shoulder, hip and knee injuries.

Triangle Pose

Aim:

The aim of this pose is to improve digestion and postural alignment by stretching and stimulating the spinal nerves.

Technique:

- Keeping your feet in the same position as the previous exercise.
- Inhale through your nose and exhale through your nose on the reach.
- Inhale and extend your arms out to shoulder level.
- Keep your legs straight and your right hip slightly stretched while lengthening along the side of your torso.
- Lengthen your torso and press your shoulders down.
- Exhale as you look along your right arm, and either with a bent or straight leg slide your arm down your right shin. Go only as far as you can without forcing the stretch.

- At the same time extend your left arm vertically and turn your head to gaze towards your extended left hand.
- Inhale and return to the standing position with your feet parallel.

Watch Points:

- If you are unable to stretch all the way to the floor you can use a Yoga Block or some other prop, or you can place your hand on your shin.
- If you have any neck issues turn your head towards the floor rather than the extended arm and soften your knees if required.

Contraindications:

- Hip, back or shoulder injuries.

Reverse Triangle Pose

Aim:

The aim of this pose is to improve digestion and postural alignment by stretching and stimulating the spinal nerves, stimulating your abdominals and lungs, stretching your hips, and opening your chest. This pose is known to ease back pain through the action of twisting and untwisting which increases the circulation of fresh blood to the discs, keeping them supple and healthy.

Technique:

- Repeat the process for the Triangle Pose that you did previously. Once you are in position, look to your right arm and inhale.
- Place your left hand down on the outside or inside of your right foot, exhale and twist from the navel and begin to turn your gaze up as you extend and reach your right arm straight up (or place it on your lower back if reaching up is too strong for your shoulder).
- Lift your kneecaps, inhale to lengthen your spine, and exhale to go slightly deeper into the twist.

- Exhale to come out of the pose.
- Inhale and return to the standing position with your feet parallel.

Watch Points:

- You can use a Yoga Block or some other prop, or you can place your hand on your shin if you are unable to stretch all the way to the floor.
- If you have any neck issues, turn your head towards the floor rather than your extended arm, and soften your knees if required.

Contraindications:

- Hip, back or shoulder injuries, and osteoporosis.
  NB: Now that you have completed this sequence of exercises, go back to Warrior 2 Pose on page 59 and do them again. This time focusing on the other side. Once you've done that you move on to the Roll Down and Balance exercise you see below.

Roll Down and Balance

Aim:

The aim of the Roll Down is to strengthen your abdominal muscles and improve the circulation of your blood. It also stretches and increases mobility in your back, spine, neck, and hamstrings. As well as releasing tension and stress, and creating space between your vertebrae, it will also improve your posture.

Technique:

- Breathing in through your nose and out through your mouth, focus on your core muscles.

- From the parallel stance of Mountain Pose, inhale through your nose and on the exhale through your mouth tighten the imaginary belt (that I introduced you to earlier) to between 50% and 70%, and drop your chin to your chest, let your shoulders drop forward, and with soft knees begin to slowly roll down toward the mat, feeling each vertebra until you reach as far as you possibly can without stress.
- Let your arms dangle and give your head and shoulders a slight shake.
- Inhale and keeping your abdominals scooped in, rise up slowly one vertebra at a time until you get to the standing position, and then rise to your toes to balance with your arms extended toward the ceiling.

Watch Points:

- Make sure you maintain soft knees on the roll down.
- Visualise each vertebra slowly moving.

Contraindications:

- Spinal injuries,
- osteoporosis,
- balance issues or dizziness,
- ankle or shoulder issues,
- detached retina.

Pilates Inverted V

Aim:

The aim of this pose, which is also known as Downward Facing Dog in Yoga, is to stretch your hamstrings, calves, arches and hands, and lengthen your spine. It also improves the digestive system and relieves back pain, headaches, insomnia and fatigue.

Technique:

- Breathing in through your nose and out through your mouth, inhale and walk your hands out to the top of the mat. Spread your fingers with your index finger forward, push the heels of your hands against the mat.
- Place your knees under your hips and have your feet hip width apart with your knees soft to start.
- Exhale and push your hips away from your hands and lift your buttocks high to make an inverted V shape.
- Rise up onto your toes and gently march one foot down, then alternate the other foot stretching the hamstrings for ten counts while inhaling and exhaling.
- Gently rise again on both sets of toes and push your heels towards the mat.

- Widen your shoulder blades and feel them move towards your tailbone.

Watch Points:

- Keep an eye on the placement of your hands.
- The pose is meant to look like an inverted V from the side view.
- Make sure you don't hold on to any stiffness in your neck, just let your head drop.

Contraindications:

- Wrist or shoulder issues, late pregnancy, high blood pressure, headache, detached retina.

The Plank

Aim:
The aim of the Plank is to strengthen your arms, wrists, spine, quads and abdominal muscles. It is particularly good for strengthening the core.

Technique:

- Breathing in through your nose and out through your mouth, transition from the Inverted V pose by walking your hands forward to make a plank with your body.
- Place your wrists under your shoulders for a narrow plank, or out to the side of the mat for a wider plank.
- The body needs to be aligned from the crown of your head to your heels.
- Try not to dip or raise your hips.
- Hold the pose for three inhalations and exhalations.

Watch Points:

- Keep your neck lengthened, your core switched on, and your hips level.
  Note: You can drop to all fours with your feet on or off the mat if the full plank is too difficult to start with.

Contraindications:

- Osteoporosis, shoulder, wrist or back injuries.

Spine Stretch

Aim:

The aim of this pose which is also known as Child's Pose is to stretch the spine, hips, thighs, ankles, shoulders, hands and wrists. This is perfect as a rest and stretch pose between all exercises, especially after the back exercises.

Technique:

- Inhale and exhale through your nose as you relax into this pose.
- Move to the floor from the Plank pose by bringing the front of your torso to rest on your thighs if possible, and your forehead just above the floor if you can.
- Either spread your knees or keep them closed depending on your ability.
- Stretch your arms out in front of your body.
- This is also an opportunity for a wrist stretch. To do this, lift your fingertips and then lift your wrists.
- Alternatively, you can keep your arms along the side of your body.
- Keep your toes rolled under for a dynamic stretch of the toes as well.

Watch Point:

- Lengthen your arms only as far as comfortable.
- Keep your knees apart if you need to, particularly if you are pregnant.

Contraindications:

- Knee or shoulder issues (although arms can be placed at the side of the body in the case of shoulder issues).
- Recent hip replacement.

Cat Stretch

Aim:

The aim of the Cat Stretch is to release the back muscles and promote awareness of the spine. It will also strengthen the wrists and shoulders, and massage the digestive organs, as well as increasing postural stability, strengthening the core muscles, and improving the circulation of your blood.

Technique:

- Inhaling through your nose and exhaling through your mouth or nose, come back onto all fours to form a Tabletop with a neutral spine and your hands under your shoulders with your legs hip width apart.
- Maintain your gaze on the mat with your neck lengthened and your spine neutral. Inhale and while you raise your chin, push your navel towards the floor as you raise your tailbone.
- As you exhale, drop your chin to your chest, arch your back and tuck your tailbone under.
- This flexion and extension can be repeated three or four times before you return to the neutral spine.
- Then roll your toes under and lift back up to Inverted V, walk your hands back to your feet, then roll up to the standing position.

Watch Points:

- Be precise with the placement of your knee and arm when you are on all fours.

Contraindications:

- Back, neck, and knee issues.

Pilates Inverted V

Aim:

The aim of this pose, which is also known as Downward Facing Dog in Yoga, is to stretch your hamstrings, calves, arches and hands, and lengthen your spine. It also improves the digestive system, and relieves back pain, headaches, insomnia and fatigue.

Technique:

- Breathing in through your nose and out through your mouth, inhale and walk your hands out to the top of the mat. Spread your fingers with your index finger forward and push the heels of your hands against the mat.
- Place your knees under your hips and have your feet hip width apart with your knees soft to start.
- Exhale and push your hips away from your hands and lift your buttocks high to make an inverted V shape.
- Rise up onto your toes and gently march one foot down, then alternate the other foot stretching the hamstrings for ten counts while inhaling and exhaling.
- Gently rise again on both sets of toes and push your heels towards the mat.

- Widen your shoulder blades and feel them move towards your tailbone.

Watch Points:

- Keep an eye on the placement of your hands.
- The pose is meant to look like an inverted V from the side view.
- Make sure you don't hold on to any stiffness in your neck, and just let your head drop.

Contraindications:

- Wrist or shoulder issues, late pregnancy, high blood pressure, headache, detached retina.

Warrior 1 and Lunge

Aim:

The aim of the Warrior 1 pose is to open your chest and increase deeper breathing. It also increases body and mind awareness and stimulates the central nervous system. The lunges strengthen the muscles in your legs while increasing your heart rate using the largest muscles in your body (the quadriceps). It is a balance, strength and stamina pose.

Technique:

- Breathing in through your nose and out through your mouth, walk your hands back towards your feet and come up to a standing position.
- From the end of the mat step your right leg back while keeping your legs and feet parallel, with your arms lengthened down the side of your body and your shoulders down.
- Inhale and lift your right heel, and as you exhale lower your right heel to stretch, strengthen and align your legs.

- Inhale again, and on the exhale lower to a lunge raising your arms to ear level. Remember to keep your left knee above your toes and your right knee towards the floor. If you have any knee pain, you can modify this pose by decreasing the bend.
- Repeat this sequence between three and five times, and on the last exhale hold, either pulse for three counts or hold for three counts.
- Repeat the whole process on the other side.

Watch Points:

- Make sure that your knee is over your toe when you are in the lunge.
- Keep the crown of your head facing the ceiling.
- Make sure that your arms are lengthened at ear level, and your shoulders are down to your shoulder blades.
- You can modify the lunge by decreasing the bend if you have any knee pain.

Contraindications:

- Knee, shoulder, and balance issues.

THE COOL DOWN PHASE

Left/Right Brain Balance

Moving on from the exercise phase, it's time to cool the body back down. The left/right brain balance is not something you'd expect to find being taught in a gym. It's all about achieving physical and mental balance by integrating both sides of the brain. What this means is that you'll be balancing your analytical and your creative capacities. This is fundamental to getting the most out of the opportunities that being alive has to offer. You'll remember earlier that I introduced you to Alternate Nostril Breathing. What I didn't make clear at that point was that breathing through the left nostril balances the right side of the brain, and vice versa. Among other things, this has a very calming effect on the body and the mind.

The Left/Right Brain Balance exercise is helpful on a number of fronts. One of those is that the simple act of turning your head while balancing on one leg helps to provide more blood to your brain, while at the same time helping to improve your balance. It breaks my heart that this exercise is not better known, and being taught to people of all ages, especially those who are not so young anymore. It is easy to do, and if it's done regularly, it could dramatically decrease the amount of falls that older people have.

Aim:

The aim of this practice is to increase physical and mental balance by integrating the left and right sides of your brain. The breath and the movement have a calming effect on the body and mind, and help to provide more blood to the brain while improving your balance.

Technique:

- Inhale through your nose and on the exhale through your mouth, take your arms out at shoulder level and draw your abdominal muscles in somewhere between 50 to 70%.
- Raise your right knee to hip level and establish your balance. Then extend your leg with a flexed foot three times. Find a point on the wall to stare at to help with focus and balance if you need to.
- Then hold your right knee with your right hand and take your knee out to the right while turning your head to the left as you breath out.
- Return your foot to the ground and repeat the two points above another two times.
- Then repeat the entire process on the other side.

Watch Points:

- Be sure to be standing tall with the crown of your head toward the ceiling, and your leg straightened without your knees locking.
- Soften the knee of the extended leg if it is difficult to hold it straight.
- Focus your eye on a spot on the wall to maintain your balance.
- Focus along your arm as your head is turned or find a spot on the left or right side of the room to focus on.
- The foot of either side can be lowered to the floor if you need to.

Contraindications:

- Balance issues or dizziness
  NB: As an optional extra, you might like to finish off with the Yoga Nidra process that I shared with you at the end of Chapter two.

CHAPTER EIGHT

THE RELATIONSHIPS WE FORM

"Only through good, true communication can you realise the joy of love."
Amy Bellows

I'm going to get right to the point here and challenge you with a call to action that might take you into uncomfortable territory. What I want you to do is fire all the negative people in your life. This is important because negative people are like cancer. They don't just make you feel terrible. They also have the power to make you sick, to age you terribly, and possibly even worse.

Mine is a 'take no prisoners' approach because as far as I'm concerned, healthy relationships are the cornerstone of a happy life. In fact, human beings are wired for connection. But not all connections are healthy. And I guess it was no coincidence that I only decided to get real with my own glaring problems with boundaries when I sat down to write this book. I say that because of course I couldn't afford to stay stuck in a dysfunctional relationship with one of my long-term friends I'll be telling you about in a moment, if I was to have any integrity around guiding people like you to focus on any areas of your life that need to be worked on. The bottom line is that sometimes we need to do uncomfortable work like this in order to be happy and well.

The long and the short of it is that I had allowed my wellbeing to be compromised by a friendship that had turned toxic somewhere along the line. When some of the turmoil that regularly flared up around this relationship settled down a bit recently, I could see that I had been in denial about the negative effect this person was having on my life.

What made this awareness so difficult for me was that I had been friends with her for decades. I was a bit like a frog who had hopped into a pot of water when it was cool and hadn't noticed the heat being turned up to the point that its skin was literally peeling off its body. The cold, hard truth of it is that the level of self-esteem I held myself in developed to the extent that the lack of respect shown to me by this friend was no longer something I could turn a blind eye to anymore. So I had no choice but to 'fire' her. In fact, it was a no-brainer to flush the person who regularly insulted me and projected blame on to me right out of my life.

The strange thing is that just after I decided I had to do something about this problematic relationship, I came across a note I'd written to myself hidden away in my wallet. It had been sitting there for a couple of years. Essentially it was an acknowledgement that I needed to do something about this person who had crossed a line with behaviour that could only be seen as bullying and intimidation. How interesting is it that it took me a couple of years to get to the point where I was able to say 'NO' to being bullied and regularly made to feel like shit.

Seeing this note again triggered some residual anger in me. This related to the fact that I had allowed this dysfunctional relationship to go on for way too long. In that moment of feeling and owning my anger, I was able to flip the anger into a feeling of liberation around how far I'd come. I share this story with you to encourage you to do the work around cutting toxic people out of your life so that you can feel liberated and free as well. Both you and I know that you deserve to save your energy for healthy relationships that nourish your soul, not unhealthy ones that make you feel unhappy and suck the positive energy out of you.

A lot of things went on in my head and in my heart as I worked my way through the very complex and emotion-laden scenario with my long-term friend. But there came a point where there was no denying that the time had come for me to let go. I don't want this to sound arrogant, but it just became clear that my energy was much better spent on helping people who are ready to be helped, rather than allowing myself to get bogged down in somebody else's negativity and addiction to drama.

What I want you to do now is reflect on whether there are any relationships in your life that are no longer serving you. If so, I want you to ask yourself what you're going to do about it. And then think about how robust your boundaries are, and whether you need to do some more work around that area of your life.

I don't know if you're anything like me, but if you are, you might be tempted to skip over any parts of a book like this where you're asked to pause for a moment of reflection and/or to take some action. If this rings true for you, I want you to know that I've written this book in the way I have to help you to take your wellbeing to a whole other level. And the way for you to do that is to fully engage with the questions I ask you to consider in an open-minded way, with a preparedness to honestly listen to what you know in your heart you need to do to get what you want out of life. So in other words, please don't skip over this.

I'm often asked what the key to my long and happy relationship with my wonderful husband is. Without hesitation I say that it comes down to open communication, mutual respect and the fact that we hold the same values. Of course, it doesn't hurt that we are deeply in love with each other, and we genuinely enjoy being together. The one thing I know for sure is that whether it's a marriage, a business partnership, or a friendship that is starting to feel like it's going downhill, when communication breaks down it's likely the relationship itself will break down soon thereafter.

My first ever romantic relationship was with a lovely Canadian guy called Ken. This resulted in our getting married when I was 21. In hindsight I can see that our union was more or less doomed from the start. For one thing I was so young. In fact, I'd never even lived outside of the family home at that stage. It's such a shame, because Ken and I were in love, and we had a lot of fun together. But before too long a serious mismatch in our communication styles became an issue, not to mention the fact that I love to dance, and Ken resisted getting up on the dance floor as if his life depended on it.

To sum the problem up, I feel like all I need to say is that I often found myself pleading with Ken to just "for the love of god, please talk to me." I'm a person who needs to talk things through, especially if there is a disagreement of any kind that needs to be worked through. The bottom line was that I simply couldn't live with someone who wouldn't sit down and talk about any issues that arose as soon as possible. And although the issue with dancing may seem relatively trivial, dancing has always been my way of staying energised, and I find it nothing short of joyful.

Not surprisingly, by the age of 23 my relationship with ken broke down leaving me as a single mum with an 18-month-old son. Ken and I shared the parenting of our beautiful little boy Shannon. He was and still is a very supportive father, even though they live on opposite sides of the world from each other now.

I found my life partner Didier four years after Ken and I separated. There's a slight irony here in terms of the importance communication holds for me. I say that because Didier is french, and his understanding of english when we met was nowhere near as good as it is now. Didier loves telling people that I just talked and talked and talked when we first met. And even though he didn't always understand me, he couldn't resist my passion and energy. That makes sense when you think about it, because it's not only words that matter when it comes to communication, things like positive energy and mutual respect count just as much (if not more) than the words that are spoken.

Another key ingredient in maintaining a great relationship is spending plenty of quality time together. A red flag goes up for me whenever I hear people bemoan the fact that their partner never wants to do anything with them. I often see these kinds of relationships go to the wall sooner rather than later. And while I know that many of us live lives that are way too busy, I have to wonder what else is going on when people say they are just too busy to make time for a 'date night' or some other kind of outing with the person they've chosen to spend the rest of their life with.

So let me ask you:

- Have you and your partner been on a date lately?
- If not, when will you schedule one in?
- If you have, did you have fun?
- If not, what could you do differently next time to have more fun?

Like most people, the first core relationship I had was with my mother. She was a brilliant and talented but ultimately frustrated woman with a particularly quirky way of thinking. Like me, she was a lover of the Zodiac. And I feel blessed to have been brought up with her Aquarian tendencies balancing out my father's more 'conservative' approach to life. That said, one of the legacies of being the fire sign Sagittarius was that my father loved nothing more than a laugh and having a great time with his family and friends. He had a lot of energy and talent in different ways to my mother. I have lovely memories of them together with mum playing the piano and dad singing during the many family gatherings we had in my childhood home in Duffy's Forest in Sydney.

When I first started writing this book, I still hadn't been able to bring myself to let go of my mother's ashes, even though I'd heard her voice in my head telling me to just "throw me to the wind." In hindsight I wonder whether my indecision about which wind to throw her to (that lasted for over eight years) was linked to my need to record the role she played in my life in the pages of a book like this one. What makes me think this, is that I was well into the process of writing about my relationship with my mother when I stumbled on exactly the right place for her to be put to rest. And I will forever cherish the memories I have of the two gorgeous ceremonies myself, Didier, our daughter Elodie, and my sister Kerri had to celebrate my mother's life under the lemon tree in our garden. I also have some of her ashes embedded in a Rose Quartz Crystal candle my son Shannon gave me a few years back. Whenever I look at this candle, I'm reminded that I have finally 'opened the gate' for my mother and myself by releasing her ashes and honouring her life and legacy in this book.

The other key woman in my life is my wonderful sister Kerri. I was totally over the moon when she was born, because all I ever wanted was a little sister to look after and play with. There she was with her beautiful blonde hair and blue eyes. As far as I was concerned. she was simply gorgeous. But it was clear that my father really wanted a boy. Oddly enough he often treated Kerri as if she was a boy, even calling her "Little Johnnie" from time to time.

None of this stopped Kerri from growing up into the wonderful strong and independent woman and mother she is today. I have reason to believe that my father was very proud of his two daughters in the end. Sadly, he isn't here to agree or disagree with me because he died way too young from bowel cancer. He was only fifty-four when he died. I can still sense his spirit here with us today, especially when I'm with my son Shannon who has a number of mannerisms that remind me of him.

My father came from a large family, and always warmly welcomed anyone who called around to visit us. He even invited one of his brother's family to live with us while their place was being built. I loved having members of the large Healy family staying with us. I have such fond memories of the many parties we had at our place. Like my parents, I'm a party person too. But I like to maintain a healthy balance if I can. I don't always get it right, but I do my best to reset the balance in my life using Yoga Nidra, and gentle movement and reflection.

As much as my relationship with my father influenced the woman I became, it's really my mother who I credit for my quirkiness and zest for life. She was a wonderful role model who filled our home with fascinating stories, and an eclectic range of friends. Among many other wonderful things, my mother gave me a lifelong appreciation and passion for music and art. She was always ahead of her time, doing things like designing ball gowns for some of Sydney's rich and famous, and travelling to places like Japan where she was invited to make gowns for Waltraud Prange who is a German soprano and the wife of Shinichi Suzuki of the famous Suzuki family.

The paradox is that as we were growing up, on the one hand my mother would be designing and making wonderful cloths and playing her beloved piano, while on the other hand she'd be acting like the dutiful wife who had dinner on the table when my father got home from work. I smile when I think about her jumping into action when she heard his car pulling up in the driveway. She would race to the kitchen to put some chopped onion with butter in a pan to give the impression that she had been slaving over a hot oven for hours. The upshot of this is that my sister and I got mixed messages. I say that because at the same time as our mother was telling us not to buy-in to the idea of being a slave to a man when we get married, she was desperately trying to maintain the facade of the dutiful wife that my father expected her to be.

I asked her about this once, and she told me it was the only way she knew of to keep a hungry man like my father quiet. I like to think that I'm pretty good at not repeating patterns like this, but I have to confess to having done something very similar with an onion on more than one occasion myself. So let me ask you - do you ever feel like you're trying to live up to someone else's expectations of who you should be? If so, does it diminish your ability to feel empowered, or does it serve as a strategy that enables you to continue to feel empowered in your own way? If not, what do you need to do to make sure you remain true to your own ideals?

What I'm getting at here is that if they are healthy, the formative relationships we have within our family not only nurture us and give us a sense of belonging, they also fundamentally shape the person we become. As you know, I was only 18 when I met my first husband Ken. I was brought up as a Catholic which meant there was an expectation that I would abstain from sex until I got married. Looking back on it now, it strikes me as ironic that for some reason I bought into this convention, while actively resisting all the other things from the Catholic tradition I didn't believe in. I guess it comes down to the mix of societal influences that I was exposed to in general, and in particular the religious doctrine that was drummed into me when I was young.

I can't help but wince when I reflect on the fact that in the 1970s when I was first married, any girl who had sex out of wedlock in the community I lived in was called a slut. This was a form of bullying that was rampant in the Catholic school system that I went through, and for all I know it probably still is.

So there I was getting married at 21 in the Catholic Church my father helped to build. When I married ken, I had just completed Teachers College and I was in my first year of teaching at a Catholic school near my home. I have lovely memories of the beautiful kindergarten children I taught scattering rose petals around us like little pieces of magic as we were getting married.

It's easy to look back over a life and wonder 'what if'. In fact, I distinctly remember my mother advising me to live with Ken before marrying him. Needless to say, my father was horrified by that idea because in his words, "only whores do that." Kerri on the other hand had already left home and was living life on her own terms. She was at art school having a wild old time. Hers was an alternative lifestyle that I often felt envious of. Why I felt bound to keep living with my parents until I got married confounds me to this day.

In retrospect it's clear to me that I was way too young to get married anyway. I really hadn't had any life experience under my belt, and on some level I knew that my marriage to Ken would never last. The important thing is that it lasted long enough for our beautiful son Shannon to come into the world. Shannon, who is now in his early forties had an incredibly difficult birth. The situation wasn't helped by my insisting that yoga and meditation were all the tools I needed to get me through the birthing process. In hindsight I can see that I struggled to have a 100% natural birth for far too long, because Shannon wound up being brought into the world via forceps that seriously damaged his little skull. I remember crying for months as I was trying to come to terms with the guilt I felt about the brutal experience Shannon had in the process of being born.

I guess I'll never know how much that guilt contributed to the severe postnatal depression I suffered from, but you don't have to be Einstein to see that it wouldn't have helped. My way of dealing with the pain I was feeling was to get out of the house as much as I could. At first, I did this by teaching fitness classes and joining a drama group. This led to my getting small parts in movies, TV shows and commercials. I also started my own drama school with a friend and acting colleague, as well as being out and about partying as much as I could. To be honest I stayed back on film sets after shoots had finished as a way of escaping the other part of my life that wasn't so rosy. This meant leaving Ken to look after Shannon a lot of the time.

I could be critical of myself as I look back on how I handled things back then, but with self-compassion I can see that I was doing the best I could with the resources I had at the time. I was still very young and way out of my depth. The fact that I didn't go under is testament to my intuition about what I had to do to get by. For his part, Shannon thrived. He appeared to be unscathed by his less-than-ideal birth experience, and his not so adept mother.

The point I want to make here is that the relationship between parents and their children must leave room for the continual evolution of the perfectly imperfect creatures that all human beings are. What I want to add is that postnatal depression doesn't have a use-by date. A lot of women, including myself, have it shadowing them for many years. And if I'm honest there's still some healing that needs to be done in this space.

The other thing that happened when Shannon was still a toddler, was that I got clear about how unhealthy it would be for me to stay with Ken. Even though he was heartbroken when Shannon and I moved out, he seemed to understand that I needed to go and find myself if I was ever going to be any good for anyone. And find myself I did. That was the time when I broke out and became the woman I should have been before getting married and becoming a parent.

I wonder if you've ever had to make a heartbreaking decision like that for your own good. Or did you choose to stay in the situation that was no good for you to avoid having to lay yourself bare to the criticism of others? In either case, I wonder if you have forgiven yourself yet? If not, what unhelpful beliefs that no longer serve you do you need to let go of to be able to forgive yourself?

Life after Ken continued to be full of all kinds of creative pursuits including my passion for dancing, watching live music, performing in bands, teaching drama and dance, getting small parts in movies and commercials, choreographing and modelling in fashion shows. Most importantly, in what people still regard as a ground-breaking move, I opened one of the first activewear shops in Australia. The piece de resistance though was starting a fitness business with my own special mix of dance and yoga. This was a big deal for me because before too long I could see that I had a gift that enabled me to make a real difference for the people who wanted to take their wellbeing to a whole other level.

Writing this now, I can see that the person I was when I married Ken was a much smaller version of myself than I needed to be to take on the hero's journey of becoming a parent. I say this because relationships can 'enable' us to be big, just as they can disempower us and keep us small. It's up to us to decide which one it's going to be. None of this is about blame. It's about taking responsibility, both on our own behalf, and on behalf of the children in our care.

One thing I can say as I reflect on those times is that Shannon and I had a lot of fun together. I loved taking him to all the activities I was involved in. Our life got even richer when my sister Kerri and her children moved in with us. Kerri even joined me in my activewear business, designing and painting beautiful unique patterns on the fabrics the clothes were made from.

This was a time when I really started loving life and having a wonderful time with my fabulous gay boyfriends. I adored them and they adored me. For the first time ever I felt like I could totally be myself. It turned out that this was the perfect space for me to be in to meet a very special person who was looking for an independent woman like me to pair up with. And that's exactly what happened. The very special person I met in 1987 is my fabulous husband Didier. He is not only my husband, but also my soul mate as well.

Shortly after meeting Didier, I made the decision to close the activewear shop and go back to teaching. I had qualifications in Special Needs Education from Sydney University, and I wound up becoming the Co-ordinator of a Centre for Hearing Impaired Children in 1989. That was also the year I agreed to marry Didier. We were married in Paris in January 1990 with Shannon by our side. This was the first of many amazing family adventures we had in Europe.

The deep love Didier and I had for each other led to my wanting to have a child with him. Falling pregnant wasn't easy this time. I took Chinese herbs for over a year to put my body into a state where conception could take place, and I eventually became pregnant in 1992 with our very special daughter Elodie. Meanwhile Shannon had become a slightly rebellious 13-year-old boy when Elodie came onto the scene. Meanwhile as tough and unsentimental as he tried to appear, I know our beautiful little girl brought as much joy into Shannon's life as she brought into Didier's and mine.

We travelled to Europe when Elodie was only 10 weeks old. And while travelling with young children can be challenging, our journeys and the adventures we had were incredibly bonding. This particular trip was followed by a settling in period as we moved into our new home in Sydney. Somewhere along the track Shannon transformed into a very caring and nurturing young man. He is currently living in Canada, and while I miss him very much, ours is one of those relationships where even if we don't see each other for a year or more, it feels as if it was only yesterday when we get back together again.

It's been a bit of a journey to get to this place with Shannon. I discovered through an Emotional Freedom Tapping (EFT) session recently that like my mother, I had developed abandonment issues somewhere along the way. Even now, the residue of this legacy can bubble up to the surface without warning, and I can feel anxious about my connection with my wonderful son. In my mother's case, her abandonment issues came out of the sense that she had been spiritually abandoned by her father when he cruelly took her horse away from her. The upshot of this is that both of us (for very different reasons) took on the belief that we have to do everything absolutely perfectly in order to be loved (and therefore not abandoned).

I remember the gut-wrenching disappointment I experienced when I found out that I hadn't won a ballet scholarship when I was 11. Through my skewed perspective, that disappointment translated into my believing that it was my body that had let me down. And through extension, I believed that I would win the scholarship and get into the school next time if I looked slimmer and prettier. What's more, I believed that because of those things I would also be loved. Talk about putting barriers between myself and being lovable!

To be honest, a side effect of this kind of all or nothing thinking can still play out in terms of my vulnerability to being triggered by things like exams and awards of any kind that I don't totally blitz these days. I guess it just goes to show that like everyone else, I'm on a journey to a place where I can love myself unconditionally. I must say I'm very grateful that I don't fall headlong into feelings of self-hatred like I used to. However, I'm not completely immune from the odd bout of perfectionism. In fact, I remember when I was being congratulated for being acknowledged as one of the top three group fitness instructors in Australia, I noticed the little voice in my head saying, "but you weren't number 1." The difference is that I noticed it happening. And because of that, I was able to stop it from eating away at my confidence and sense of achievement.

What I know now is that I was always talented, and that I am accepted for who I am and what I have to offer to the people who live, love, and work with me. It's an exciting and deeply satisfying stage of my life that I'm in right now. That doesn't mean I'm superhuman. I still need to be mindful and catch myself whenever negative thinking starts to raise its head. Another example of the residue of my past relates to catching myself projecting my longing for 'success' (whatever that means) on to my daughter. To cut a long story short, there was a part of me that desperately wanted her to be famous. It was more than a mother wanting their daughter to get what she wanted.

In hindsight I can see that I was hanging out for the vicarious glow of success to shine over me. To that end I was putting a lot of pressure on Elodie to put herself 'out there' more than she was at the time. I always say that awareness is power, and all I needed was to become aware of what was going on to get out of that headspace and recognise that it isn't fair for Elodie to have to carry the burden of my desire to bask in the glory of her fame and/or success. In that moment, I was able to make a conscious decision to let that go and relax in the knowledge that Elodie's journey is hers, and my journey is mine.

This is a brilliant example of the way patterns repeat themselves across the generations until someone heals enough to be able to let go and evolve. I've had decades of personal development work to thank for being able to look back with compassion on my mother who was desperate for me to become super successful and famous in the dancing and fitness arenas. It was as if my success could make up for the fact that she was never able to live up to her own potential. I'm very grateful that this pattern is now broken thanks to the healing and self-awareness work that I've done on myself over the years, and more recently through the process of writing this book.

There's no doubt that relationships can be tricky. That's why having great communication skills is so important. I feel really blessed to be able to maintain an open and honest line of communication with my kids. For example, Elodie recently told me she left school harbouring the belief that she was not very smart because one of her teachers told her that she would be better off in one of the lower classes. This belief stayed with her for years until she got up the gumption to go back to study at university and found out to her great surprise that she is actually very intelligent and talented in many ways. What a wonderful breakthrough that was for her.

My hope is that hearing this and the other stories that I've shared with you in this chapter will help you to identify any relationships and/or stories you're telling yourself that are stymieing you in one way or other.

What I know for sure is that it is the connection with kindred spirits that brings a special kind of magic to my life. Collectively we create joy, and we create a place where we feel like we belong on a very deep level. The Body and Balance tribe I invited you to join earlier at bodyandbalance.com.au is full of great people drawn from all walks of life. They represent a wide range of ages, occupations, shapes and sizes. But they share a common passion around striving to achieve a sense of balance in their body and their mind.

The pivot I made in 2020 to keep this tribe thriving involved turning my living room and studio into a live streaming space. That way I was able to continue to teach my classes when we went into lockdown because of Covid. Because of the way things have panned out in Australia where I am based, I've been able to bring back face to face classes as well, but I'm also now able to cater to an international audience via my live streamed and recorded options. I'm really excited about what lies ahead as I prepare to take my programs into the corporate world, as well as launching an elite suite of programs for women who are ready to step up and leave behind anything that is holding them back.

What I want to say is that if anything you've read in this chapter has agitated you a bit, it's time for you to look at the quality of the relationships you have with the key people in your life. This of course includes the relationship you have with yourself. I've got two things to recommend if you're not sure how to go about this. The first one is to take the advice of his holiness the Dalai Lama who is well known for telling people to spend some time alone every day. The other thing I want to recommend to compound the effect of spending time with yourself, is to regularly tick off things you've been wanting to do but have been putting off for some reason.

What I want you to do right now is to think of one thing you could act on this week. Then write down the action that you've resolved to take and put it somewhere where you'll see it every day. It doesn't have to be anything massive. It might just be about buying yourself a beautiful book to start a daily awareness diary in. Or it could be about regularly taking a walk outdoors, or starting a class, or embarking on a project like writing a book, or sailing around the world. Just tap into your heart and see what comes up for you when you think about this.

Of course your 'thing' might be more of a 'no-thing'. It might be about sitting for 10 minutes and reading a magazine you've been wanting to read for a long time, or finding a few minutes to meditate, or something like that. Then at the end of the week I want you to reflect on how you feel now that you've taken the initiative to start doing something for yourself.

It's important to keep doing what you started so that the benefit of this small initiative will start compounding. So, schedule your 'thing' into your routine. It's the small things like this that can transform your life over time. And once you've done one thing, it will be much easier to slot in another one when you're ready. And before you know it, you will be starting to feel a real sense of inner satisfaction, peace and accomplishment from the cumulative effects of the small steps you've taken to care for yourself.

I have an example of my own I'd like to share with you here. A while back I subscribed to a magazine that I really enjoy reading. It's the simplest of simple treats that I look forward to every week. It means the world to me because my busy schedule involves teaching every day, and always being on my feet. So my weekly indulgence of sitting down with a cup of tea and my magazine full of gossip, fashion, and stories of drama and love, allows me to make myself a luscious cup of tea and spend time in the peaceful space that I set up especially for this activity. This might not seem like such a big deal to you as you're reading about it here, but for me it is a big deal because I've always found it difficult to justify having downtime. The fact that I have a weekly reminder to stop and take time for myself in the form of a magazine arriving in my letter box has had wide ranging implications on my sense of wellbeing, and the relationship I have with myself.

From my own experience and the feedback I get from my clients, this kind of simple intervention can be revolutionary. In my own case it enabled me to see that the only thing stopping me from doing little things for myself was an unwillingness to give myself permission to put time aside for treats in my schedule. Once I gave myself that permission, I started to feel free. So let me ask you - what do you need to give yourself permission to do right now?

CONCLUSION

This book represents the ultimate gift of service that I feel blessed to be able to offer to people who are moved to read it like you.

My hope is that you will do the exercises peppered throughout the chapters. These are my invitation for you to open your own gate, because you see there is no lock on the gate to personal freedom and abundance. The gate is just sitting there waiting for you to open it. And all you need to do now is to be brave, fearless and light-hearted as you open the gate for yourself right now.

Writing this book has enabled me to acknowledge and honour my lifelong passion for movement, people, health, wellness, longevity and personal freedom. What's more, through writing it I've finally been able to open the gate to personal freedom I've been seeking my whole life.

I firmly believe that once we finally let go of whatever it is that's holding us back - whether it's a poor self-image, or being stuck in relationships that no longer serve us, or emotional baggage of one kind or other, we will be able to access the abundance that is our birthright.

What I'm going to leave you with is my much-loved mantra and call to action that I finish off all the classes I run with. I feel like these words might contain the message that will help you to change the course of your life forever.

To prepare yourself, I invite you to lie in a relaxed, quiet space, and visualize something positive you would like to happen for you, your family, your friends, or the universe. Then:

- **Say it to yourself.**
- **See it.**
- **Feel it.**
- **And make it happen.**

Do this three times every day, and I promise that you will shift your energy in a positive way.

Here's to your success.
Jill Healy-Quintard.

APPENDIX I: SHORTCUTS TO BEING WELL

1. **Improve your digestion:**
   If your food is not working for you and/or you have a weak gut, it will negatively affect your body and mind. Things like weight gain, sleepless nights, brain fog, and more negative outcomes are likely to result. Supporting sound digestion involves being strategic about what you eat and giving your body some balanced enzymes. You might like to consider taking a daily probiotic to maintain a balanced gut.
2. **Support strong gut health:**
   An effective immune system depends on a healthy gut as well. When it comes to gut health, probiotic supplementation is not just a good idea, it's absolutely crucial. It will bring your intestinal environment into a more balanced state by repopulating the supply of friendly, helpful bacteria.
3. **Reduce stress:**
   Stress causes our cortisol levels to rise. Chronic, elevated cortisol can lead to all sorts of problems including weight gain, anxiety, sleep disorders, and hormonal imbalance. Because we live in a world full of stress, I want you to remember that you have several breathing exercises in chapter seven that will help you to bring your stress levels down. And you can't beat taking yourself outside in the sunshine for a decent fast paced walk or doing some other kind of exercise to bring the cortisol down and the feel-good endorphins up. Establishing a regular practice that encompasses stretching, muscle balancing, core conditioning, cardio and Yoga Nidra Meditation will predispose you to remain in a balanced state, even when things that would have otherwise stressed you out happen.
4. **Get enough sleep:**
   Your natural circadian rhythms help regulate your hormones. But the world we live in is not particularly conducive to avoiding the things that make it hard to get a good night sleep. This is a problem because a lack of sleep can cause

hormonal fluctuations that have the potential to throw your whole system out, and seriously undermine your health in the process. If you're like way too many people in the world who struggle to get 7 to 9 hours of quality sleep per night, I recommend you start experimenting with things like:

- Practicing Yoga Nidra before going to bed.
- Limiting your intake of caffeine after lunch.
- Drinking camomile and other relaxing teas.
- Consuming things containing tryptophan such as milk and baked potatoes prior to going to bed.
- Ensuring that your screen time finishes at least an hour before you go to bed.

1. **Use natural skin care products:**
   Many skin care products are made with harmful chemicals including DEA, parabens, propylene glycol and sodium lauryl sulphate. All these things will increase the toxicity in your body and potentially trigger hormone problems. So, look for natural, organic products that are free of these kinds of toxins.

2. **Be mindful of how you prepare your food**
   Avoid plastic bottles, aluminium cans, and containers that are not BPA-free. BPA is the chemical that makes plastics solid. The problem is that it has toxic effects on the body. So, it's worth buying glass or stainless-steel refillable water bottles and storage containers if you can't find BPA-free options, and switch from non-stick cooking pans to stainless steel, ceramic or cast-iron pans.

3. **Consider bio-identical hormone replacement therapy:**
   Bio-identical hormones are compounded to suit the specific needs of peri-menopausal or menopausal women. They are safe, plant-based compounds that are identical in structure to our body's own hormones. I've been using bio-identical hormone replacement therapy for a number of years now. The great thing is that they don't pose any of the risks that synthetic hormones do.

4. **Look for alternatives to medications:**
   It's worth discussing other options to the commonly used medications like antibiotics, birth control pills or other medications you are on with an alternative therapist because there are always side-effects to putting chemicals into our bodies. That's not to say that you should never take antibiotics when you have an infection, I just want to urge you to keep your mind open to alternative options to keep yourself well using natural products such as fish oil, and probiotics to maintain a strong immune system.

5. **Support liver function:**
   Drink a large glass of room temperature water with a squeeze of fresh lemon juice every morning to give your liver a daily boost. Apple cider vinegar is also helpful as a liver detox, and if you're daring and like a little spice, you could try a spoonful of turmeric powder in warm almond milk with a dash of pepper.

6. **Strive to buy organic meat, eggs, and dairy:**
   The only 100 percent fool proof way to avoid hormones in your food is to buy organic meat, eggs, and dairy.

APPENDIX II: CASE STUDIES

Pamela Knight came to my classes back in 2007 and loved the passion and energy of these classes. She moved away and returned recently and found me through my website and booked a ZOOM consult to discuss her current Fitness and Wellness requirements.

Pamela said: "Jill Healy Quintard is a welcome Beacon of Light when navigating the often, murky waters of the Fitness Industry. In a post-covid era of so many Self – proclaimed "Experts" who sometimes have no more claim to fame than a Tik Tok video, it was refreshing to meet up with Jill. Jill is a Coach who can back up every claim with qualifications, knowledge, experience, and her enviable passion for Life. She is committed to developing her clients in a Holistic and healthy way to be the best version of themselves. Jill has been in the fitness industry for many years and has the Industry awards to prove how highly she is regarded. I have no doubt that her teachings have inspired many, many, clients over the years and the impact of training with Jill has encouraged hundreds to lead healthier lives."

Lisa Trewin has been working with Jill since 2004. She contacted Jill because she was experiencing problems with thoracic and hip imbalances and a weak core.

Lisa said: "I've been a Jill devotee for close to 17 years. I'm passionate about Body and Balance! Especially Jill Healy-Quintard style......Jill's energy is phenomenal, and addictive. Even on those days when you don't want to exercise, you know her energy and the company of the classmates will lift your heart and your endorphins.

It's this energy that keeps me motivated. Jill's newsletters and social media posts are also very encouraging, educational and inspiring."

Tracey Smail started attending Jill's *Body and Balance Pilates* classes because she was experiencing lower back pain, and she was looking for a group class to take with like-minded people.

Tracey said: "I have been attending Jill's 'Body and Balance' classes on and off for 18 years. During that time, I've met a great group of ladies that I feel a real affinity with. Jill is an enthusiastic and incredibly positive person who motivates us all by her passion for movement, dance, yoga, Pilates, and the idea that we must all keep moving for balance and agility. She is an inspirational and motivating teacher, advocating the benefits of exercise and attitude for a greater quality of life. She is a wonderful asset to our community and is truly a great mentor to us all."

Mandy Blackburn started attending Jill's Pilates classes almost 20 years ago. She was motivated to start because she wanted to increase her fitness and core strength.

Mandy said: "I've participated in Jill Healy-Quintard's varied classes for almost 20 years, trying everything she offers from Tribal Dancing to Pilates. My personal favourite is her Pilates/Yoga Nidra class where she teaches us the importance of building core strength whilst having fun in the process. Jill builds a sense of camaraderie and social interaction through her classes; She refers to this as "finding your tribe".

Jill is a natural leader, passionate about what she does, sharing her extensive knowledge of health and fitness to skill people up to lead a healthier, more active life. She uses this gift to organise and participate in many charity and social events, as well as organising workshops, and offering personalised one-on-one personal training for those who are just starting out, or those with particular conditions they need to focus on. Jill also puts together a very informative newsletter with a delicious healthy recipe to try every month.

Jill has won many well-deserved awards for her huge contributions to the health and well-being of others."

Phil Bee started attending Jill's classes because he wanted to maintain his fitness in general, and flexibility in particular, so that he could continue to enjoy his numerous sporting activities and the physical work he likes to do.

Phil said - "I've been doing Pilates with Jill for about twelve years now, and I know that it is what I need to do to be able to keep up with the activities that are a big part of my life. I've reached the level of Black Belt 1st Dan in Karate, as well as playing hockey and surfing. I know that it's Jill's Pilates classes that keeps my core strong enough to keep surfing at my age. I also love the camaraderie in all of the classes with the great crew of men and women who enjoy Jill's style of teaching.

Pilates is extremely beneficial for me because it is a low impact way to strengthen my core, as well as stretching and toning my body, with a focus on flexibility. This sets me up to maintain my fitness and continue with my surfing and hockey. Pilates also involves rather precise moves and specific breathing techniques. I really enjoy doing Pilates with Jill and hope I can continue with it for many more years."

Melanie Macfarlane started attending Jill's classes 5 years ago after the birth of her baby. She was keen to regain core strength, flexibility and relaxation for her busy mind.

Melanie said: "I have been attending Jill's classes for around 8 years now and I am so glad I found her. I actually met Jill at an event when I was pregnant. She noticed my flushed and puffy face and encouraged me to rest and consider having some tests done. As it turned out, I had pre-eclampsia and required total rest. I'm so grateful that Jill took the time to notice and cared enough to say something to me. When my now 9-year-old was a baby, I decided to start classes with Jill to build my core strength and flexibility.

Her passion and enthusiasm in every class and the workshops that she runs is contagious. I feel a sense of joy and connection with the community of like-minded people I meet at every one of Jill's classes. Her classes are totally inclusive and non-judgemental. She encourages everyone to do their best and is mindful of everyone's needs. This comes down to Jill's brilliant teaching ability, knowledge and experience. I love the fusion of Yoga and Pilates as well as the added cardio with weights and the beautiful relaxing Meditation at the end of every class that Jill runs. What's more, Jill has the best music. This is also very motivating....... we all want Jill's playlists."

Lucy Tildesley: Lucy has been coming to Jill's classes for almost 4 years. During this time, she contracted breast cancer and needed surgery. Jill worked with Lucy during that period helping her with specific exercises to regain her strength.

Lucy said: "Jill Healy-Quintard is a unique, inspirational exercise instructor who provides plenty of details so that we all know what we're meant to be doing. This is one of the things that makes Jill's classes so enjoyable. She also cultivates a friendly, welcoming environment, with great music, fun routines and she even adds lavender to the eye pillows we wear for the Yoga Nidra relaxation session at the end of every class.

Jill's classes make me feel better! She was very supportive while I was recovering from surgery 2 years ago."

Sue Fortescue: Sue began Pilates classes 8 years ago. She was keen to improve the lower back pain she was experiencing and gain core strength and flexibility.

Sue said: "Thank you for the classes that have changed my life and helped me to be part of a new community of people. Thank you also for the marvellous, uplifting experiences gleaned from your Joy, Love and Gratitude 1/2 Day Retreat. I am still "on a high" and have learned so many valuable life skills, not to mention the benefits I gained from sharing the fellowship of the other participants.

My gratitude has no bounds thanks to you Jill. I will definitely be attending your next 1/2 day retreat, "Exercise for Face, Mind and Body" because the first 1/2 Day Retreat I attended, "Scripting the Future", along with your Nidra Yoga, have made me into a new person and ensured that I will not be missing out on any of your truly valuable life lessons to come."

Maggie Weir: Maggie started attending Jill's Pilates classes to help with the stress she was experiencing. She knew Jill was the person for her because she had been a student of Jill's dance/drama class with a Yoga Nidra component when she was in Primary School.

Maggie said: "I am new to Body and Balance, but I am loving it – thanks to Jill and everybody for being so welcoming! I first came to meet Jill many years ago when she ran a class for the students of the school I went to. This was my first introduction to Pilates and who knew that Learning Jill's Yoga Nidra technique would end up having such a big impact on my life. I found the systematic relaxation strategy invaluable during my stressful teenage years and as a tool to combat insomnia. I am currently in my final semester at university, and I am enjoying Jill's Pilates classes immensely, and I look forward to continuing it in the months to come."

Therese Stafford: Therese has been attending classes for 5 years. She started because she was experiencing lower back pain.

Therese said: "Jill is a dedicated, professional and caring instructor, who can lead a class and simultaneously provide specific exercises tailored to individual's needs and limitations. She has extensive knowledge of the human anatomy as well as a deep understanding of mind body balance. She fuses fitness and wellness with her passion for using movement as medicine, keeping us Baby Boomers feeling and looking fabulous.

I love Jill's A45plus Pro-age Empowerment App that let's women like me follow a program that covers classes from Beginners to

Advanced, with weight loss tools and meal plans - all delivered with Jill's motivation."

Katherine and Simon Navin: Katherine and Simon have been doing Jill's classes for 16 years.

Katherine said: "When Covid 19 and Lockdown hit, Jill started Live Streaming her fabulous classes. Previously both Simon and I had only done one class a week. Now we do 2 to 3 and have never felt or looked better. Even our massage therapist told both of us how toned our muscles had become, and when Simon went to a boy's football reunion in Newcastle, his mates told him how strong and fit he looked. Simon told them that it all comes down to Jill's classes, particularly BodyBarre, which he said is harder than footy training.

Thank you Jill for being such an inspiring role model for so many."

Annie Straiton: Annie has been doing Jill's classes for 6 years.

Annie said - "I feel so lucky that I have been able to continue Jill's classes anytime I wish. I have had some health issues, and I'm often tied up looking after grandchildren. I particularly love the YogaPilates Fusion and the BodyBarre in the Online Pre-recorded sessions as they can be done in a small space, and I get a wonderful workout."

Ariella Kaplan: Ariella is doing Jill's classes through her A45 Plus Pro-age Empowerment App.

Ariella says: "There are so many things to love about the A45 Plus Pro-age Empowerment App. I haven't exercised for more than five years... and I was finding it hard to get motivated until I found this app. My biggest challenge was that I 'never had time' but I can't use that excuse anymore. The app has videos that are anywhere from 5 minutes to 20 minutes long and include single exercises and full classes. I can take these exercises and do them at work or anywhere when I find myself with 10 minutes free. I love that I can track my progress daily, and I've gone from not being able to do five squats, to now being able to do 50 per day. I've lost inches and my clothes are loose. Walking used to be painful but now I walk daily.

The weekly Zoom calls with Jill are very targeted and motivate me to stay on track, and the nutrition guides are also excellent. They are really simple to follow. I can highly recommend this to anyone, especially women over 40 who may be challenged by symptoms of menopause... I've found that exercise helps to alleviate many of the symptoms. If you've been thinking about exercising and not sure where to start... start here."

THANK YOU TO MY SISTER KERRI FOR THE BEAUTIFUL, SPECIAL AND MEANINGFUL ARTWORK.

Sensureality Art House
Kerri Anne Healy

www.ingramcontent.com/pod-product-compliance
Lightning Source LLC
Chambersburg PA
CBHW050315010526
44107CB00055B/2251